FROM TEENS TO TWENTIES

From Teens to Twenties

Lessons Every Young Adult Should Learn

ALEX BASILE

ST PAULS

Library of Congress Cataloging-in-Publication Data

Basile, Alex.
  From teens to twenties: lessons every young adult should learn / by Alex Basile.
    pages cm
  ISBN 978-0-8189-1371-6
 1. Teenagers–Conduct of life. 2. Young adults–Conduct of life.
3. Teenagers–Religious life. 4. Young adults–Religious life. I. Title.
  BJ1661.B439 2014
  248.8'3—dc23

                          2014008183

Produced and designed in the United States of America by the
Fathers and Brothers of the Society of St. Paul,
2187 Victory Boulevard, Staten Island, New York 10314-6603
as part of their communications apostolate.

ISBN 978-0-8189-1371-6

Current Printing - first digit   1   2   3   4   5   6   7   8   9   1 0

Place of Publication:
2187 Victory Blvd., Staten Island, NY 10314 - USA

Year of Current Printing - first year shown

2014   2015   2016   2017   2018   2019   2020   2021   2022   2023

TABLE OF CONTENTS

Table of Contents

While reading the works of Alex Basile, it becomes evident that Alex has a solid understanding of the value of faith in our culture. Culture shapes the human person. When faith is intimately connected to culture, we thrive as individuals, made in the image and likeness of God, within a community rooted in God.

When this does not occur we find ourselves wrapped in the "cloak of narcissism" created by our own ego within a community of isolation and unhappiness.

What happens when the culture divorces faith?

What happens when the culture is apathetic to faith?

What happens when the culture is afraid of faith?

The answer is we live without God. As someone once wrote, "Life without God is like an unsharpened pencil, it has no point."

Yes, life without God is meaningless. Young adults need God and this is the very reason that Alex Basile was inspired to so carefully craft the "Lessons that Every Young Adult Should Learn." In my estimation this is a book, not only for the young, but also for the young of heart who want to grow in a deeper faith amidst the challenges of a secular culture.

Alex tries to wake the reader up to the obvious when it comes to the challenges of faith in culture. Did you ever imagine that...?

+ A relationship with God will have an impact on every relationship in your life?
+ The only energy that we put into our faith lives is attempting to avoid it?
+ The "Comfort Zone" mentality prevents moral and spiritual growth?
+ The culture of "on line" communication teaches that "when no one is looking, anything goes"?
+ It is becoming more impossible each day to censor the "nonsense" out of our world?
+ Education begins when we ask questions that touch our faith, morals and culture?
+ Our world has chosen entitlement rather than gratitude?

After the French Revolution, the founder of the Marianists, Blessed William Joseph Chaminade found himself in a culture in France where people no longer had the faith. This was a culture that consciously removed faith from the human experience. Imagine a generation or two that never had one Christmas, no Baptism, no first Holy Communion, and no Church. Father Chaminade believed that he could restore faith to culture by working with youth, for they were then, and are now the future of the Church.

Alex Basile was formed in this tradition as a high school student and now as a Catholic educator in the Marianist tradition. He has great hope in the youth of the Church and so has given us these essential lessons so that young people be empowered in keeping the faith in Jesus Christ in our culture.

Father Thomas A. Cardone, S.M.
Chaplain, Kellenberg Memorial

INTRODUCTION

Being a theology teacher in the 21st century, I am obligated to do much more than simply teach students about God. I have always attempted to make the connection between God and living a life of happiness and joy. Existential lessons creep their way into every class. Some of these serve as practical reminders of how to act and what to do as we live out our days. Other reflections have been presented to assist my students in altering the way that they think about certain subjects.

Some of the greatest knowledge has been handed on to me from those who have lived more years than I have. In turn, I have tried to return this favor to my students. It is my hope that you will also be able to benefit from these lessons. Although I teach religion, you need not have an expansive knowledge of the Bible to gain something from this book. I only ask that you approach each reflection with an open mind. Many of these ideas came from the discussions and debates that have evolved in my classroom.

We hold onto our opinions like old friends. After years of them being with us, we do not even give a second thought to their validity. It is for this reason that I have written this book. Every once in a while, we must take stock of our beliefs and our standards of living and determine whether or not these things must change. Education begins with asking questions, so never stop asking, "Why do I act the way I do?", and "How can I change to make my life better?"

We are like pieces of clay that are molded by the people we meet and situations that we face. I implore anyone I know that a relationship with God enhances this process. Each day should be another step in the learning experience of becoming fully human. This book will discuss the alternatives that society will offer to reach this end. Our culture may dangle many tempting carrots but there are no shortcuts to true happiness. We must work on improving ourselves as well as our relationships.

If you're not a religious person at this point in your life, I beg you to keep reading. I will not preach, but rather, offer simple advice. Without God, life is meaningless, so we must consider Him as part of our discussion. Only a few of my students continue to argue with me about this fact once they have heard my complete argument. Most self-help books attempt to guide their readers without including God because some people grow uncomfortable with spiritual discussions. I make no excuses for something that I believe is necessary. A relationship with God will have an impact on every relationship in your life. Everything improves once we have our hearts in heaven.

Self-actualization begins with introspection. We have the ability to change into people who know what we want and understand where we are going. We think that we have life all figured out when we realize that we really do not know the person who stares back at us from the mirror. We spend our time looking outward and forget to peek inside. Some of our greatest self-knowledge is acquired from others. It is vital that we learn from the advice (and maybe even the criticism) from those who know us best.

There are many optional paths as we walk through life. The road to fulfillment and happiness is not guaranteed to be the smoothest one. Sometimes the rocky road forms us into who we are meant to be. I hope the advice and suggestions in the following pages are helpful to you. These ideas were formed not only by research but also through the joys, laughter, heartaches and sorrow I have experienced. Share the possibility of an extraordinary existence by changing your unhealthy habits that deter you from truly relating to others. I have used this quote by C.S. Lewis as a personal motto, "Self-sufficiency is the enemy of salvation." We must rely on our relationship with God. As Jesus stated, "I am the vine, you are the branches. Whoever remains in me and I in him will bear much fruit, because without me you can do nothing" (Jn 15:5). No matter what happens in life, He is willing to help us bear the load. On Good Friday, Jesus demonstrates that He can carry His cross and ours.

Sometimes we are our own worst enemy. We need the help of God and others in order to survive. Open your heart and mind to see life from another perspective. Use your relationship with God to fortify your other relationships. Build a life with Christ that will bear much fruit. Make these years of formation the strong foundation that you can build upon the rest of your life.

Biblical Abbreviations

OLD TESTAMENT

Genesis	Gn	Nehemiah	Ne	Baruch	Ba
Exodus	Ex	Tobit	Tb	Ezekiel	Ezk
Leviticus	Lv	Judith	Jdt	Daniel	Dn
Numbers	Nb	Esther	Est	Hosea	Ho
Deuteronomy	Dt	1 Maccabees	1 M	Joel	Jl
Joshua	Jos	2 Maccabees	2 M	Amos	Am
Judges	Jg	Job	Jb	Obadiah	Ob
Ruth	Rt	Psalms	Ps	Jonah	Jon
1 Samuel	1 S	Proverbs	Pr	Micah	Mi
2 Samuel	2 S	Ecclesiastes	Ec	Nahum	Na
1 Kings	1 K	Song of Songs	Sg	Habakkuk	Hab
2 Kings	2 K	Wisdom	Ws	Zephaniah	Zp
1 Chronicles	1 Ch	Sirach	Si	Haggai	Hg
2 Chronicles	2 Ch	Isaiah	Is	Malachi	Ml
Ezra	Ezr	Jeremiah	Jr	Zechariah	Zc
		Lamentations	Lm		

NEW TESTAMENT

Matthew	Mt	Ephesians	Eph	Hebrews	Heb
Mark	Mk	Philippians	Ph	James	Jm
Luke	Lk	Colossians	Col	1 Peter	1 P
John	Jn	1 Thessalonians	1 Th	2 Peter	2 P
Acts	Ac	2 Thessalonians	2 Th	1 John	1 Jn
Romans	Rm	1 Timothy	1 Tm	2 John	2 Jn
1 Corinthians	1 Cor	2 Timothy	2 Tm	3 John	3 Jn
2 Corinthians	2 Cor	Titus	Tt	Jude	Jude
Galatians	Gal	Philemon	Phm	Revelation	Rv

FROM TEENS TO TWENTIES

The only way to be a Christian
is to be like Christist

People seldom recognize the Bible as the greatest love story ever written. Instead, many interpret sacred Scripture as a complicated book of rules and regulations. The story of the Bible is actually quite simple: God created the world so that He could love us and we would love Him in return. The story reaches its apex when God sent His Son to live among us. Jesus became human so that we could have an example to follow. Jesus would show us how to live, how to pray, how to love and find fulfillment even in the insanity of our world.

As Christians, we focus on the practical matters of our faith. We worry about when we are obligated to attend Mass; we contemplate how often we should pray; we manage how much money we should give in the collection on Sunday; we calculate how often we sin. Although we search for the secret formula in living, the answers stand right before us: we need to be like Jesus. We clog our lives with many alternatives, but there is no substitute for the real thing. From the moment that we were able to speak, we learn to talk a good game. We create an excuse for every situation. The only energy that we put into our faith lives is attempting to avoid it.

Jesus spent many hours preaching, but in the end, He reinforced everything He said with His actions. He experienced the confusion of humanity firsthand. Jesus demonstrated that the most powerful antidote to the temptations of this world is loving others. Every action of Jesus abounds with devotion to other people. In a culture where we measure people by their popularity and power, we will do anything to reach the top rung on the ladder to success. Jesus showed that we should take a different path to true fulfillment. Swiss theologian Philip Schaff explained how the love of Christ overshadowed every other figure in history with His simple approach to life.

> Jesus of Nazareth, without money and arms, conquered more millions than Alexander the Great, Caesar, Mohammed, and Napoleon; without science and learning, he shed more light on things human and divine than all philosophers and scholars combined; without the eloquence of school, he spoke such words of life as were never spoken before or since, and produced effects which lie beyond the reach of orator or poet; without writing a single line, he set more pens in motion, and furnished themes for more sermons, orations, discussions, learned volumes, works of art, and songs of praise than the whole army of great men of ancient and modern times.

Jesus set the bar high for us. Message after message He complements His words with amazing love. After His last earthly words were spoken, we were left with the perfect pattern of living. When in doubt, flip through the Gospels to witness His never-ending care for others.

Jesus was sent from heaven to show us that in giving ourselves away, we receive the most. We shall talk more about this in depth later. Jesus fought through pain and weariness for our sake. He spent countless meals sitting with the lost and lonely because He was worried about their souls. Being a Christian demands that we live as selflessly as Jesus. If we consider the well-being of others in every action, we will live according to His will and discover true fulfillment.

We experience tremendous joy during Christmas as we give to others. The benevolence of God does not cease as we put away the decorations until next December. We, too, must continue to place others at the forefront of our lives. Every day we will embrace the warmth and joy of that blessed season when we give ourselves without limits.

Jesus put a new spin on doing things "on our own terms." Through betrayal, Jesus demonstrated understanding; through mockery, He displayed forgiveness; through ignorance, He instilled wisdom. There will be many situations when we may insist that some people around us are too unlovable. Jesus upends everything and changes our perspective on every relationship. He urges us to love at every opportunity.

Since we are never beyond the reach of God's mercy, He asks humanity to also extend our arms as He did on His sacred cross. Jesus shows us that everything we do is of consequence. The smallest action affects the people around us. Because of our connection to Him nothing is random. We are called to act as if everything we do involves Him. To be a true Christian, we must do everything in our power to infuse the love of Jesus in all of our relationships. Look to Jesus to find the strength to love even when you feel that love is not possible. Others will know your association with the Teacher by your compassion and kindness. Wear Christ in your attitude and style. Spend each day trying to be like Him and you will unlock the greatest secrets of this life.

The main obstacle keeping you from a relationship with God, is you

As a teacher of theology, I spend my days pondering and debating the God question. I encounter students at various levels in their faith. In every class there are usually students who makes their feelings quite clear: they refuse to believe. Sometimes the students put their complete faith in science and leave God out of the equation. Sometimes they state that God can't exist with all of the suffering in the world and sometimes they simply do not take the time to look into the question.

I always remind my students that no one stands between God and us, but us. We put on the blinders that keep us from recognizing His presence in everyday life. Faith is similar to love in that we choose to love. We must also choose to believe. Even if we pile up all the evidence we can find, we will never prove the existence of God with absolute certainty. If we wait for the magical moment to occur when we see the manifestation of God through some bright light, we may be left standing in the dark forever.

Having a relationship with God requires us to open not

only our eyes, but our hearts to Him as well. As His name Yahweh implies, He is all things, to all people. He is love, mercy and forgiveness. He is laughter, tears and joy. He is the author of Scripture and nature. God is so complex, we may never truly understand who or what He is.

We spend our time obsessing about our earthly pursuits. God stands beside us but we fail to recognize Him because we are either too busy or do not care. Rather than looking to God, we put our faith in alternative gods. We chase riches, power, beauty and other foolish dreams as a replacement for the emptiness in our lives. We search for tangible rewards that instantly fulfill us. Rather than waiting for our eternal reward, we are content with momentary bliss. Henry David Thoreau, American author, poet and philosopher, urged us to substitute this fruitless pursuance with an effort to discover God: "The smallest seed of faith is better than the largest fruit of happiness."

The modern Christian approaches worship as another means of gratification instead of an act of self-giving. We mutter, "I didn't like the music" or "The homily was boring," as we leave church on Sunday. People lose sight of how worship should help us to please God. Going to church is a vital part of our relationship with the Lord as we seek communion with Him. Remember, you are the one who determines when or if you will attend Mass. You are the only one who can pour your heart into prayer. No one else can do these things for you.

Growing into adulthood means that we are given more freedom. We have the ability to turn to God or turn away from Him. As Pope John Paul II said, "Freedom consists in not doing what we like, but having the right to do what we ought." God has created us to love and honor Him. Use every iota of your evolving freedom to worship God with of all your heart, mind and soul.

Adoration can only begin when we are conscious of God. Cast aside your doubts, resentment, fear and anything else that is keeping you from a real relationship with your Creator. Get out of your own way and move closer to God. His presence will become more apparent when you are willing to see Him. Use every day to work on the relationship that will fulfill you in this life and in the next.

You've got to be in it to win it

How many times have you quit something before you have even begun? In a quick fix world, we seldom have the patience to work on a particular skill or sport. We desire to become instant experts without any effort. Many of us forget that even the experts were once novices. We are mesmerized by the talent of the artist or athlete and assume that they were born with their God-given ability. No one witnesses the endless hours shooting foul shots in the gym or the crumpled pieces of paper that hold the drawings that were not adequate enough. Instead, the world falls in love with the glory of victory and the flash of the spotlight.

When you start a new job others may exhale impatiently when a routine task is difficult for you. As you sense a colleague's frustration, you may contemplate running for the nearest exit. The first days, weeks or even months in a new endeavor can be painful. Remember that no one can keep you from success if you are determined to succeed. No one else is able to determine your potential. Allow this sentiment of Winston Churchill to echo in your mind when you hit a roadblock: "Never, never, never give up." Don't let the naysayers talk you out of your dreams. Keep pushing forward. None of the greatest ideas or inventions would have ever come to fruition if people didn't think outside the box. Skeptics called Columbus and Galileo "insane" because of their revolutionary thinking and adventurous spirit. They were ridiculed and ostracized during their lifetime, but today we hail them as heroes.

Once we throw in the towel, any chance at victory vanishes. It is impossible to score a touchdown when you stand on the sidelines. There is no substitute for hard work and perseverance. Success occurs when a person sees the light on his darkest day. Basketball superstar Michael Jordan summed up his own career:

> I've missed more than 9,000 shots in my career. I've lost almost 300 games. 26 times I've been trusted to take the game winning shot and missed. I failed over and over again in my life and that is why I succeed.

Even in the midst of resistance and pain, those who are willing to forge ahead have real hope of reaching the finish line. Set goals for yourself.

Never hesitate to dream big, but be realistic. If you faint at the sight of blood, it may not be in the cards to become a surgeon. You should look to utilize your talents. Hard work has tremendous benefits. Your talents are waiting to be revealed to the world. Your potential can enable you to do great things. Great empires were not built overnight. They took the efforts of many people. The greatest success can only occur with serious effort. Famous American statesman and inventor Ben Franklin said, "There is no gain without pain." Don't let the small setbacks derail your dreams. If you desire something badly enough, be willing to deal with some heartache along the way. Success is sweetened when we are able to overcome our disappointments. Stop doubting your potential.

The same is true when it comes to faith. We want the great light to appear to illuminate our doubts and fears. When Mother Teresa said, "God doesn't require us to succeed; he only requires that you try," she had more than career expectations in mind. She spent many hours on her knees in prayer pleading for a glimmer of faith when disbelief consumed her.

Imagine the grief and distress of the apostles after the death of Jesus. They quickly ran and hid in the upper room where only a few days earlier they had celebrated the Passover feast with their friend and teacher. With the members of Christ's inner circle locked away, the new Church was bound to fail. It was not until the Holy Spirit provided the gifts needed to spread the gospel message that the apostles emerged from their cocoon to begin their evangelization. The apostles are a beautiful example of what happens when we move from the sidelines to the action of the game.

The apostles must have been inspired by the determination of Jesus. He had many reasons to quit on the road to Golgotha. Every step with the crushing cross on His already battered shoulders was excruciating. Jesus left a lasting image with the members of the newly established Church. Push yourself and see how far you can go. The greatest things in life come to us with diligence. Standing on the sidelines will keep you yearning for more. Get in the game!

Dating is not a contact sport

My students often talk about their social lives on the weekends. They speak nonchalantly about how they have "hooked up" with a particular person. Dating in the 21st century has taken a new approach to relationships. Young people today jump into physical relationships before they really know someone. Rather than building a relationship on friendship, today many relationships are built on the shaky ground of superficial attraction. Our culture that thrives on instant gratification says, "Don't wait. Get what you can to please yourself."

We all crave love and attention. Unfortunately, sometimes we will do anything to feel wanted. The "hooking up lifestyle" leaves people with even more unanswered questions than before they have entered into their latest sexual experience. We become attached to the object of our physical experience and wonder why the phone does not ring or the other person does not wish to engage in another encounter. We end up even lonelier than if we had not been involved with another.

I recently sat with a student, James, who expressed his

frustration with the social scene. At seventeen years old, he had grown weary of the mind games that he felt that most people played. Every Monday, after another weekend of various encounters, he would see the girl or girls with whom he had been involved with over the weekend. James wondered why these girls did not seem to pay any more attention to him than before their experience. He desired to find a girl who appreciated him as a person.

I challenged James to avoid "hooking up" and evaluate how the young women he met perceived him. I stressed that it is impossible to truly get to know a person without any true communication. James and I spoke at length about how friendship must be at the heart of the physical relationship if it will reach its fullest potential. The main component of friendship is love. Without friendship, people may enter relationships thinking only of themselves. James returned to my office to express his amazement at my "playing hard to get" strategy. Without the haze created by his empty sexual encounters, he could now focus on the true person.

In a culture that focuses on physical appearance, we overlook the inner person. I encourage James and all my young friends to court rather than date. I remind them of the days when people had to learn to love when faced with a prearranged marriage. Young people were not given the freedom to choose their own spouse. Courting was a period of getting to know one another under the supervised eye of another person. You learned how to relate to your future spouse while you gained knowledge of who they were. When you date as if someone is watching, you hopefully forego the empty pursuit of the physical for a search of the authentic person.

Many of my students argue about the value of sexual experience before marriage to measure the compatibility of a couple. I quickly point to the staggering rise of divorce rates and sexually transmitted diseases. The way we approach our relationships is destroying the family and worse yet, killing us.

Our culture argues that two consenting adults have the right to express their love with sexual intercourse. In his book, *The Good News About Sex and Marriage*, author Christopher West explained how it is only through the nuptial covenant of marriage that this union is made valid:

> At the moment they give their consent, the bride and groom are fundamentally changed. They become right then and there (and only right then and there) husband and wife. What did not exist five minutes before does exist now – a marital bond sealed by the Holy Spirit that once consummated, can never be dissolved by anything but death.

Simply put, when you love enough to have sex with another person you should contemplate the vows that can seal that relationship for a lifetime. The value of marriage has been diminished by our society. We approach marriage as we do when purchasing an item from the department store. If we are not satisfied, we simply return the object and begin our search again. Married life offers us the possibility of entering a relationship that elevates us as human beings. Sexuality is at the core of this sacred bond.

The sexual relationship of a loving couple was meant to be special. As a matter of fact, it was given to us as a way of experiencing heavenly ecstasy. Sexual intimacy for a married couple can be magical. When we wait until marriage for sexual intercourse, we will reap the benefits of chaste life. We must seek the virtue of chastity. Chastity advocates the goodness of sexuality. It helps us in pushing away lust, which lures us into treating others as objects. Lust also presses us to use our sexuality for our own selfish desires and not to truly love others. Sexuality is meant to be self-giving rather than self-assertive.

Listen to the encouraging words from St. Paul on the splendor of love:

> Love is patient, love is kind. It is not jealous, love is not pompous, it is not inflated, it is not rude, it does not seek its own interests, it is not quick-tempered, it does not brood over injury, it does not rejoice over wrongdoing but rejoices with the truth. It bears all things, believes all things, hopes all things, endures all things. Love never fails. If there are prophecies, they will be brought to nothing; if tongues, they will cease; if knowledge, it will be brought to nothing. (1 Cor 13:4-8)

Build friendships when you date. Enjoy the people you meet as you get to know the true person. Seek to give rather than to receive. Replace your feeling of sexual desire with the craving for the completeness of love. Put the long-term needs of the other person ahead of the desire for instant gratification. Discover the true pleasure and ecstasy within the heart of another. You will experience the incredible joy of a sexual relationship when you find your one true love. It is the one true gift that gets even better when you wait for it.

Life is not a loophole

A loophole is defined as "a means of escape; an ambiguity or omission in the text through which the intent of the statute, contract or obligation may be evaded" (*Merriam Webster Dictionary*). Many people use loopholes to beat the system. Great lawyers have made their living on finding loopholes in the law and winning cases for their clients. There are many reasons why we take shortcuts: weariness, laziness or perhaps apathy. Some people live by the motto: "Live smarter, not harder." Society may insist that we can live by our own code, but we cannot avoid the truth. The culture of relativism allows us to make up our own rules as the game proceeds. We ignore the truth in favor of our own subjective will.

The loophole mentality blindly frees us from any responsibility. When the pressures of life threaten us, we sometimes search for an easy solution. I recently caught a student cheating on their final exam in my class. Cheating is a problem, but cheating on a religion test is a deep moral dilemma! The parents and students all explained that the testing irregularity occurred because of too much stress caused by a heavy workload. We can make all the excuses we wish, but we must never overstep our responsibilities.

Modern medicine has progressed amazingly over the past fifty years. Recently I saw an ad promoting a new birth control pill that interrupted a normal monthly cycle and caused a woman to menstruate only four times a year. The commercial asked, "Who says a woman must have her period once a month?" I thought the answer to this question was quite simple: God. The modern world does not hesitate to interfere with natural law. We desire to change things because of inconvenience. Some truths are unavoidable. We can rationalize aborting an unwanted pregnancy by insisting that a fetus is not really a child; we can have several drinks and insist that we are fine to get behind the wheel of a car; we can redefine marriage to suit our sexual desire; but it does not change the reality of the objective truth.

Truth is bigger than us. It existed long before Moses brought the Ten Commandments down from Mount Sinai. Many people insist that we can reinvent the truth when the situation dictates. I spend many days teaching my students the truth of Jesus and the Church He established. Some of my students dismiss my lessons as my opinion. They fail to understand that I did not sit in my room and come up with these rules and laws. Remember, opinions are only as valid as the evidence that back them up. Once we understand this important fact, we can find the secret to understanding the major issues in society.

When we turn on the television each day, we see politicians debating both sides of an argument. Each side attempts to draw support from the strength of their oratory skills. They forget that no matter what you say about an issue, you can't escape the truth. Author Michael Novak warned about the danger of relativism:

No great, inspiring culture of the future can be built upon the moral principle of relativism. For at its bottom such a culture holds that nothing is better than anything else, and that all things are in themselves equally meaningless. Except for the fragments of faith (in progress, in compassion, in conscience, in hope) to which it still clings, illegitimately, such a culture teaches every one of its children that life is a tale told by an idiot, signifying nothing.   (*National Review*, April 2005)

As Christians, we look to Jesus as our moral compass. He called Himself "the Way, the Truth and the Life." He shows us the path to the Father. He reveals the ultimate reality of this world. He provides breath in this world and the next. Jesus also reminded us that there is no easy way to God except through Him. Many people have attempted to find an easy way to heaven and a relationship with God. Jesus demonstrated that true discipleship could cost not just something, but everything we have. Read about the lives of the apostles and witness the sacrifice they made for their relationship with Christ.

When you are lost and need to determine your path, you can look to Christ to give you direction and discover the objective nature of things. Live your life by a higher authority. Live by truth and not subjective opinions. Be mindful that you cannot elude your responsibilities. An honest and fulfilling life is one without loopholes. Keep it real.

You get more flies with honey

Have you ever been so frustrated that you wanted to scream at the people connected to your situation? There are many scenarios in life in which we must rethink our approach to others even when we know that they may be the cause of our problems. We may certainly have every right to argue our case, but in the end, we may not get the results that we desire. My parents taught me to live by the old adage, "You get more flies with honey." They understood the value of a gentler exchange between people.

When differences exist between others and ourselves, it is best to hear what other people have to say first. It is easier for others to listen to criticism after they have had a chance to unload their feelings. We do not want to make others perceive that they are inferior to us. They will find comfort in knowing that they face the same challenges as us. When people are put on the defensive, their egos are bruised. They fear embarrassment. Communication usually helps us to defuse a tense situation.

Always commend a person before you make a recommendation or criticism. Individuals feel valued when a conversation begins on a positive note. When you recognize a person's strength, he or she will feel a greater connection with you and be more open to see your opinion.

It is always prudent to walk away from arguments that you cannot win. When others are blind to the truth, adding your own opinion may possibly alienate them all the more. When the time is right and the water is less turbulent, you may venture into the subject area by gently mentioning objective facts related to your original argument. When your "opponent" listens to the facts away from the battlefield, he or she may be more receptive to the alternative point of view.

Putting yourself into the shoes of another may open your eyes as well. Find a common denominator with the person you are trying to win over. This may allow you both to see the situation from the same point of view. Strive to comprehend the other's perspective and motivation. This can permit you to feel the similar thoughts, emotions and experiences of each other.

We should always keep the possibility that we may be wrong in the back of our mind. People often state their opinions dogmatically without any room for revision. We can learn something new every day if we are open-minded. Be willing to re-examine the facts, rationally. Admit your mistakes quickly so that everyone can move on. Nothing blocks progress like obstinacy. Do not hesitate to poke fun at yourself when you are wrong. Humor enables everyone to find the lighter side of the situation. You may even disarm the most serious of subjects.

One of the most popular prayers urges us to enter each situation with the heart of Jesus. "The Prayer of Saint

Francis" recommends that we work to reverse difficult situations and cultivate a world where kindness and compassion prevail. Every situation and circumstance will benefit from this approach:

> Lord, make me an instrument of your peace.
> Where there is hatred, let me sow love;
> where there is injury, pardon;
> where there is doubt, faith;
> where there is despair, hope;
> where there is darkness, light;
> and where there is sadness, joy.
> O Divine Master, grant that I may not so much seek
> to be consoled as to console;
> to be understood as to understand;
> to be loved as to love.
> For it is in giving that we receive;
> it is in pardoning that we are pardoned;
> and it is in dying that we are born to eternal life. Amen.

Jesus exhibited the proper way to deal with those going down the wrong path in life. Preaching and harsh words were seldom necessary. Criticism is the last thing a person needs to hear when a heart is hurting and an ego is bruised. Jesus knew the power of common ground. Others responded to Him because He made every encounter about them.

You will win many people over with a softer and sweeter approach. The hardest of hearts will melt when you display your warmer side. If people respond to the "honey" that you have doled out, then you have won them over. If they reject you, then at least, you have demonstrated how others should act when faced with disagreement. It is difficult to respond negatively to a smiling face. Enter into all your encounters with a friendly demeanor and see an immediate change in the way that others respond to you.

Life exists beyond the weekends and vacations

Some days it is more apparent than others. I am in the middle of teaching my class and I see their eyes starting to glaze over. Some students do not try to hide their boredom. The frustrated artists start doodling. The eyelids of the chronic narcoleptics begin to shut. The shifty eyed clock-watchers commence the countdown until the end of class.

Especially in the early hours of the school day, the front of the classroom can be a lonely place for a teacher. Apathy manifests itself in the heart of many of the high school seniors that I teach. Because of the demands of school and their obligation to attend, many students begrudge being there. They wish away the hours of each day. We tend to live by the clock philosophy. People watch the hours of the clock move in a circular motion. One day melts into the next. We wake up each day and feel that we did the same exact thing the day before. Because of the endless repetition of the clock, we allow boredom to set in unchallenged. We forget that life is cumulative. It travels in the vertical direction instead of the circular motion we see on a clock. Each event affects the next. No moment is wasted.

As soon as we begin school in September, we look forward to Christmas. In March, we count the months until summer. Starting each Monday, we wish away the days until the weekend. As a culture, we seldom enjoy living in the present. We constantly anticipate something bigger and better. We long to be in a place where the lights are brighter and the pace is faster. Being from New York (the city that never sleeps) I feel the effects of being on the perennial treadmill. Today the big-city mentality of running constantly has crept across America.

Young people cram so many activities into one day. Schoolwork is pushed later into the evening. New age technology allows young people to communicate quietly into the early morning. The bloodshot eyes of the average student bear witness to their busy schedules. The chaotic nature of the average day makes our young people long for a day off when schedule is lighter and there is a greater opportunity for sleep. As I tried to coax my students from their catatonic haze, I urge them to savor the more mundane moments of life. These are the unexciting occasions away from the buzz of the Saturday night party and the stimulating times with friends. These are the days where boredom buzzes around us like a pesky fly. Young people seem to dread the days when they are not entertained constantly.

There are simple tasks and everyday responsibilities that become exhilarating when completed with great joy. A person should treat each day, as it is, a gift from God. Avoid facing each day as a chore that must be accomplished. When you wake up each day, I encourage you to ask yourself the following:

1. What are my goals for this day?
2. What did I learn yesterday that I could utilize today?
3. What can I do to show my family and friends that I love and appreciate them?
4. What might I be thankful for today?

Face each morning with gratitude and anticipation. Use it as an opportunity to inspire others through your quiet strength. Mother Teresa said, "Be faithful in small things because it is in them that your strength lies." Away from the fanfare and hype, God calls you to see the extraordinary in the humble, the magnificent in the mundane and the glorious in the obscure.

Enjoy each moment and stop rushing your life away. There will be a time in your life when you long for the more simple times. Use the saner moments to reflect on your relationships and how you can improve them. Live in the present. Learn the importance of contentment and peace of mind. Practice service to others through kindness and patience. Shift your focus from the calendar and the clock to others. Every second of your life on earth will have greater meaning.

Live life like the camera is rolling

When people channel surf, they immediately realize the amount of reality shows that are on television. This type of programming fascinates people. We watch people as they attempt to become the next superstar or supermodel. We observe how people survive on a deserted island. We are glued to the television as people search for the perfect husband or wife. The networks promote a type of voyeurism that monitors the lives of people as they deteriorate before our eyes. The more dysfunctional the show, the higher ratings seem to soar.

People volunteer for reality shows because they yearn for instant fame. They dream of the spotlight that will hopefully also bring them instantaneous celebrity status. These people don't seem to mind having their reputation damaged as long as material wealth and popularity follow. All is sacrificed for the sake of notoriety. Some young people have mimicked this mentality by posting some of their most outrageous moments online. They allow the world to have an inside peek at the lunacy that occurs on the weekend away from adult intervention.

Reality programming and life on the internet contradict how the average person usually reacts to the camera. When placed before the lens, we usually primp in attempt to perfect our look. We try to show the world our best. No one wants the camera to capture the disappointments and the heartaches of life. The pictures displayed on our mantles depict the Kodak moments when life is at its sweetest. We stand arm in arm with the people that we cherish the most on the happiest occasions of our life. As the photographer raises the video or digital camera, arguments are replaced by smiles. Our difficulties are pushed out of the picture for the time being.

But the average person acts differently when they think that no one is looking. Years ago, I owned a delicatessen. You would often see a person drop money out of their wallet. Unaware that the money was missing, they proceeded to place their order and wait for it to be completed. Occasionally the person next to them in line would alert the person that they had dropped the money. But other times, another customer would attempt to put the money into their pocket. When a clerk from behind the counter intervened, the person who took the money acted as if they had no knowledge of whom it belonged to.

We sometimes morph into people who have forgotten about integrity and morality. Once we are out of the public eye, anything goes. We no longer care about the rules and regulations. We neglect the well being of others and the environment around us. It is only when we feel that there are eyes upon us, we snap back into line. Once the sun goes down, the behavior of some of our most solid citizens begins to change. Statistics show that most juvenile crimes occur during the evening. We sometimes do the unspeakable when no one can see us.

In the Gospel of John, we hear about people who leave the presence of Jesus and enter the faithlessness and despair of the dark. A corrupt Judas sought consolation in the depths of the night. He attempted to hide in obscurity because he knew that the light would bring attention to his disgrace. The lack of light can't cover our shame and the betrayal of truth and goodness.

We should approach life as if someone was capturing our every move. Consider these questions: If our parents were looking over our shoulder when we were on the computer, would we avoid certain images and web sites? If an adult were present when we hung out with our friends, would we still do the things that we do? Am I honest about how I acted with my girlfriend or boyfriend when we were with their parents?

True role models act as if someone is always watching. This is how they are able to inspire and influence others. When pictures of Michael Phelps surfaced of the Olympic champion smoking pot, a debate ensued over whether this incident affected the swimmer's status in the public eye. Many of my students argued that Phelps' personal life should not affect his professional career. But Michael Phelps became a role model not only because of his heroics in the swimming pool, but because many people, especially children, admired him as a human being. When we start to separate the real person from what he or she does, we move into dangerous territory.

Living each moment as if someone is scrutinizing our every move can be a real challenge. We are lured into the darkness where the view of our actions is obscured. Dwell in the light and be proud of your every deed. Be the example that others may follow any time, and everywhere. Make your life a reality show that is filled with love and compassion. People will tune in to witness the example of how to truly be.

Death is inevitable.
Stop acting horrified when someone brings up the subject

For three weeks each February, I teach the section of the senior religion course on death and dying. We watch segments of Bill Moyers' series *On Our Own Terms* that he produced for PBS. I explain to my students that the videos deal with patients who are facing terminal illnesses. The students are unexpectedly shocked when each segment ends with the death of the patient. Even when we know that death is imminent, we have a tendency to deny the inevitable.

Most people avoid the subject because they fear the unknown. Each Christian who reads the Bible hears the incredible promise of eternal life, yet we fail to be reassured by the words of Jesus. Instead, we fret over the finality when this earthly existence has ended. We obsess over the relationships and situations left behind by our death or the death of a loved one, even though the reward of heaven goes well beyond the possibilities of this world.

Many students face the effects of death for the first time when a grandparent dies during their high school years.

Suddenly, death becomes a reality. A person that they love deeply is gone. They must deal with the overwhelming feelings that loss incurs. They are not sure of what to say or do. They look around themselves to see how others deal with death. Their own grief becomes accentuated by the way their parents deal with their loss. Their grief can become our grief.

For the first time they may realize that death is not merely an event, but a process. A world that seems to fall apart comes back together with the help of time and love. Even when we attempt to keep death in the distance, it has a way of entering our lives when we least expect it. The more we deny it, the harder it comes crashing into our lives. Our desire to ignore death makes it even more difficult to deal with when it occurs. We would rather speak about anything besides death. People reveal their most intimate secrets, but yet the subject of death remains taboo. Horror movies depict the morbid nature of death. They sensationalize the gore and blood associated with a violent death. It makes for a great thriller, but presents a portrait of death that does not fit well into our ordinary lives. This unrealistic portrayal makes us avoid the subject altogether.

The subject of death should provide a learning experience for people of all ages. It should make us appreciate life. Each day, each breath, and each sunrise should give us enormous pleasure and joy as we experience them. German poet and novelist Hermann Hesse said:

> The call of death is love. Death can be sweet if we answer it in the affirmative, if we accept it is one of the great external forms of life and transformation. Saying "yes" to death is actually a "yes" to life.

34

Even though country music is not as popular in New York as in many of the other parts of the United States, every one of my students is familiar with the Tim McGraw song "Live Like You Were Dying." The chorus of the song makes us contemplate the many things we have yet to accomplish:

> I went skydiving
> I went rocky mountain climbing
> I went two point seven seconds on a bull named
> Fu Man Chu
> And I loved deeper
> And I spoke sweeter
> And I gave forgiveness I'd been denyin'
> And he said some day I hope you get the chance
> To live like you were dyin'
> (*Nichols, Wiseman and Craig*)

The reality of death should make every person reconsider his or her plans for the coming day. It should cease the postponement of simple tasks and the procrastination of the things that need tending to. Death moves our relationships to the forefront of our priorities. It awakens us to cherish the time that we have together. Some people put together a "bucket list," an agenda of things to accomplish before dying. If we live each day as if it were our last, we will not hesitate doing the things we really want to do. Each moment will be filled with the passion it deserves.

Death should also make us reevaluate our relationship with our Creator. With God, death is not an end, but the beginning of our new life. The famous preacher Billy Graham said:

I have a certainty about eternity that is a wonderful thing, and I thank God for giving me that certainty. I do not fear death. I may fear a little bit about the process, but not death itself, because I think the moment that my spirit leaves this body, I will be in the presence of the Lord.

Without God, death is finality and nothingness, but if we believe in Him we can live forever. Death opens the door to His everlasting kingdom.

Make your discussions on death focus on its positive qualities. Death urges us to discover the beauty of this life as it serves as a bridge to the next. The inevitable nature of death makes it part of every person. It is an undeniable and essential quality that we can't avoid. Comfort those who sorrow and allow others to console you in times of despair. Take nothing for granted. Listen to the words of Jesus and be prepared at all times:

> Then the kingdom of heaven will be like ten virgins who took their lamps and went out to meet the bridegroom. Five of them were foolish and five were wise. The foolish ones, when taking their lamps, brought no oil with them, but the wise brought flasks of oil with their lamps. Since the bridegroom was long delayed, they all became drowsy and fell asleep. At midnight, there was a cry, "Behold, the bridegroom! Come out to meet him!" Then all those virgins got up and trimmed their lamps. The foolish ones said to the wise, "Give us some of your oil, for our lamps are going

out." But the wise ones replied, "No, for there may not be enough for us and you. Go instead to the merchants and buy some for yourselves." While they went off to buy it, the bridegroom came and those who were ready went into the wedding feast with him. Then the door was locked. Afterwards, the other virgins came and said, "Lord, Lord, open the door for us!" But he said in reply, "Amen, I say to you, I do not know you." Therefore, stay awake, for you know neither the day nor the hour.

(Mt 25:1-13)

We know neither the time nor the place when the Lord will call us home. Open yourself up to death and live each day as if it is a glorious gift.

A kind word can change someone's day and even their life

As human beings, we often feel that we are powerless to change the world. We imagine ourselves standing on the shore with a tiny shovel attempting to keep the tide from rushing in. Human beings underestimate the ability that God has given us to touch the heart of another. As we go about our ordinary routine, we bypass the opportunities to stop and interact with the people along the way.

Everyone experiences feelings of abandonment and loneliness periodically. We have our moments when we think that the world has forgotten about us. There are people around us who deal with loneliness every day. These are the people who long for conversation in the cafeteria or in the office. They hope for a phone call when an invitation will finally come. As illustrated in the very first pages of the Bible, people were not meant to be alone. God acknowledges this in the creation story as He says, "It is not good for the man to be alone. I will make a suitable partner for him" (Gn 2:18).

Mother Teresa understood the desperate nature of loneliness. She said, "Loneliness and the feeling of being unwanted is the most terrible poverty." The amount of interaction desired may vary from person to person, but no matter who you are, a certain amount of contact with others is required to find fulfillment and happiness.

A person does not have to be a prisoner in their house or deserted on an island in order to feel the effects of loneliness. There are plenty of souls who feel abandoned while in the midst of the classroom, school hallway or busy mall. People want to be recognized. They yearn to be heard. Jesus spent His ministry confronting the loneliness of the sinner. His greatest gestures of love may have been the moments involved in simple, yet engaged conversations with the lost and abandoned. We can learn much from the interaction of Jesus with others.

There are many reasons why people have become lonely. The slope of decline may have been gradual for some into the world of separateness. Some have dissolved into the realm of loneliness because they may have expected too much from the people in their lives. Others may send forth negative signals that repel others. People can undermine their relationships by unconsciously sabotaging them. Others may have grown tired of working on their relationships. Some individuals build barriers because they believe they are unworthy of love. Once the walls are in place, few people want to take the time and effort to knock these walls down, both from inside and out.

We tend to leave people to their own devices, because we naturally are more concerned about our own well-being. We go about our daily business and miss the empty and brokenhearted people in front of us. The first step in reaching out to others is awareness. People must be able to sense what is happening around them in order to make a difference in this world. We become so wrapped up in ourselves that we forget others exist. We have all experienced a situation where people have walked past us as if we were not even there. Encounters like this can immediately change our perspective on our self-esteem.

Realize the importance of not only opening your eyes, but your heart as well to others. I often tell my students the key to popularity is not being interesting but being interested instead. We are usually concerned with how others view us. We worry about self-image and keeping up appearances. We become obsessed with the superficial exterior. However, the greatest work takes place on the inside. People wait for the moments when they can unveil their deepest longings and concerns. Look people in the eyes when you ask them, "How are you?" In our culture, these words have become a greeting rather than an indication of heartfelt concern. Truly listen to hear the response.

Use a person's name when you speak to them. Ask them about specific people and events that are important to them. Take the time to focus on the people in front of you. Put away the distractions that inhibit true communication. Make a real connection with others.

Another important aspect of communication is demonstrating that you empathize with another. We should show others that we understand what they are feeling and that we are sensitive to their innermost thoughts and emotions. William Shakespeare spoke about the need for empathy:

And tell them that to ease them of their griefs,
Their fears of hostile strokes, their aches, losses,
Their pangs of love, with other incident throes
That nature's fragile vessel doth sustain
In life's uncertain voyage, I will some kindness do them:
(Timon in *Timon of Athens*, Act 5, Scene I)

The seeds of kindness grow long after you plant them. One solitary act of compassion can lead to many others. It costs absolutely nothing, except time, to stop and say hello to someone. Everyone wants to be acknowledged. Take a moment to share a compliment to make others feel good about themselves. Allow another to cut in front of you in line at the store or in traffic. Hold open the door for the person behind you. Drop a coin in the parking meter that has expired. Individuals want to be recognized for their self-worth and when strangers receive kindness, they are likely to do the same for others. Your act of kindness will continue to evolve and grow long after you exit the situation. A true Christian heart flourishes when we look out for the needs of others.

Use your power to change the world. Be attentive to the lonely and lost. Invest in your fellow human beings. Take on the attitude that there are opportunities to alter your surroundings and the general demeanor of others. Your own outlook will change as well. Start the process today with one simple act of kindness and watch miracles occur.

There is a big world out there, experience it

Every person has a comfort zone. We live within our comfort zones because they are safe. We stay in this territory because we know what to expect. As a guidance counselor, I would wait for the sophomores to return from lunch on the first day of school. The panic was evident in their eyes as they lined up outside my office. When I asked how I could help each student, they explained that they wanted to move their lunch period because none of their friends were with them. Sadly, I told the students the reality of the situation was that I could not change their schedules. I also explained that this presented an extraordinary situation to meet new people and possibly make new friends. As they left my office dejected, I sympathized with my young friends. We gravitate to people we already know when we enter social situations. I am guilty of this myself. But when we deny ourselves new experiences and the opportunity to venture into uncharted territory, we impoverish ourselves.

We are creatures of habit. We eat at the same restaurants; we shop at the same stores and may even vacation in the same places. We hate change. We would rather be numbed by complacency than exhilarated by the thrill of new experiences. Soldier and statesman Colin Powell explained the philosophy of those stuck in the world of obsequious serenity:

> "If it ain't broke, don't fix it" is the slogan of the complacent, the arrogant or the scared. It's an excuse for inaction, a call to non-arms.

It is ironic that as people who love surprises, we journey each day through life as if we dread the interference of anything unexpected. We choose, instead, to calculate every move.

My parents taught me the value of travel at a very young age. We journeyed to simple places that gave us a break from the ordinary routine. These days created memories that will last a lifetime. I know many people who find traveling a hassle. It is certainly easier to avoid the packing, the long lines for security and tight seats on an airplane. But seeing Rome, Paris or the Grand Canyon for the first time takes your breath away. These are the things that you will never experience from the comfort of your couch.

Some people avoid being locked in a car with family members because they fear what can happen when left in confined quarters with certain people. We may be surprised how a relationship can change when we experience new things together. Travel opens us up to new possibilities. It gives us knowledge of other cultures and people. It helps us to break the monotony of our usual routine and at the same time gives us a new awareness of the things that we may take for granted.

Boredom consumes us because we fall into our habitual routines. Our world grows smaller and smaller because we are self-limiting. The menu constantly expands but we choose the same things to eat. At the next party have a conversation with someone that you have never met. Sit at a new table in the cafeteria to encounter others that you would normally never speak to. One of the most common statements I hear while on retreat where people are forced out of their comfort zone is, "I can't believe how nice he or she is!" After months or even years of seeing someone in the hallway or in the classroom from a distance, everything changes. It is amazing how our perception evolves with each new experience.

We have all had someone pass food to us and urge us to try a delicious item. We politely refuse and stick with our favorites. My parents would always say, "You will never know what you like, if you do not try new things." Let this be your motto when you are challenged to venture down different avenues.

Think outside the box. Make a list of the things that you would like to accomplish. Try a new hobby. Spend time learning a new language. When people ask why you would do these things respond, "Because I can!" You need not make excuses for traveling down new roads. Life is a journey in which we are forever evolving until the day that we die. We will never grow unless we are open to new experiences. Expanding your horizons will change the way that you think and live. Start new chapters of your life by entering the unknown. We may not know where each door leads, but we will never find out until we open it. Leaving the comfort zone requires some courage because it involves risk. The security blanket shields us from allowing the unknown world from seeping into our ordinary lives.

Christian discipleship requires going outside of ourselves. Jesus spent most of His time with the wretched and forgotten. Keeping company with these misfits drew the attention of the popular crowd. Becoming involved in these social circles instantly shattered the comfort zone of Jesus. Jesus made no bones about reaching out to these people. He offered no excuses. There will be times when friends scoff at your relationships. The hand of Christian love needs no rationalizing.

The young bird discovers that it must leave the safety of the nest in order to fly. We must leave our comfort zones in order to soar. God has given you the wings, go and fly on your own!

Embrace the classics, you may learn something new from the past

I always want my students to be aware about how new technology has changed from when I was a child. My students are amazed that I was able to survive on only seven channels and even more astounded that I would enjoy a program that was not in color or high definition. When I show them clips from old black-and-white movies, their initial groans subside when they get drawn into an interesting plot. We often feel that we live at the pinnacle of civilization and believe that our innovations enable us to produce the greatest inventions and artistic creations ever.

Being in a band for more than twenty-five years, I think I have figured out the songs that draw people to the dance floor. Each year the band provides music for an event called the Junior-Senior prom. Students volunteer to spend an evening with residents from a nursing home facility and act as escorts to the dance. The most fascinating aspect of the evening is witnessing an eighty-year-old and a sixteen-year-old singing the same song.

I always define a "classic" to my students as something

that stands up against the test of time. The emotional awakening that it evokes enhances the timelessness of art. A classic speaks to each generation with the same intensity as the one before. When a song invites the listener to tap his foot or sing along even years after it premiered, it may be considered a classic. When people desire to see a movie over and over and still relate to the plot even though its language and dress have long gone out of style, it may be a classic.

Our society cherishes the latest and greatest and the new and improved. We search for the latest fad or trends. When we want a book to read, we look to the best-seller lists. We turn our noses up at the "stuffy" old classics. My eleven-year-old son recently told me that he refused to listen to music recorded before 2005. We quickly discard the items with a few nicks and scratches once more attractive alternatives appear.

A classic never goes out of style. Edith Wharton defined a classic in this way:

> A classic is classic not because it conforms to certain structural rules, or fits certain definitions (of which its author had quite probably never heard). It is classic because of a certain eternal and irrepressible freshness.

People of all ages experience the same emotional rush when listening to Frank Sinatra or the Beatles and when watching *The Sound of Music* or *It's a Wonderful Life*. A classic makes us feel good about life even when we know the plot by heart and can recite the lyrics in our sleep. When we look back at classic music and movies, we often forget that the people who created this art had to work with less technology than we have available today. Instead of working in front of a computer, they spliced pieces of audio and video taped together by hand. They generated special effects through pioneering techniques that set the stage for the innovations that we take for granted today. Even if we do not appreciate a person's art, we should admire them for the time and commitment that they spent perfecting their craft.

Scientist Carl Sagan explained, "You have to know the past to understand the present." Our love of the classics should lead us to a deeper appreciation of what we have today. We spend a large amount of class time studying history. The purpose of looking back is to improve our sight as we look ahead. As author Aldous Huxley stated,

> The charm of history and its enigmatic lesson consists in the fact that from age to age, nothing changes and yet everything is completely different.

Our dismissal of the classics is indicative of the way we treat the older people in our society. We forget that anyone who has lived for more years than us possesses invaluable wisdom through their experience. The cosmetically enhanced world views wrinkles as flaws instead of the "beauty marks" from truly experiencing life.

Our school spends countless hours at assisted living facilities and nursing homes. Sitting with a senior citizen aids us in seeing the world from an entirely new perspective. We are immediately transported back in time. A conversation with an older person enlightens us in ways that no textbook could ever do. Sit down with the living classics in your world.

Soak in the glory and joy from the time spent on earth. Learn from their mistakes and tribulations.

The Church always honors the classic people in its history through the veneration of saints. When a devotion to a particular holy person continues well after their death, they are considered for canonization. As we study the classics, we must not overlook these men and women who have withstood the test of time through their holiness and relationship with God. The saints show every person how to find joy even though they may have lived through difficulty. Centuries may pass, but we are bound to these people through their goodness and benevolence. These ordinary people show the possibility of living an extraordinary life. The saints exemplify that anyone can experience a radical transformation no matter who they are or how they have lived in the past.

The classics bridge the old with the new through timelessness. They make us appreciate another time and place. Learn from the things that age but never grow old. Make the classics a part of your life. Sing the best songs. Watch the best movies. But most of all, learn to live from people who have discovered the secrets of living. Embrace the classics.

Sometimes "no" means I love you

We learn from the time that we can remember that perseverance is our best friend. Even if our parents were not willing
to purchase the object of our affection, we would wait for
the opportunity when they might change their mind. It is
amazing how young children possess the instincts to know
when their parents' resistance is weakest. Children ask and
continue to push mom or dad until they are ready to say
"yes."

Parents today work harder than ever to give their children the best that life can provide. I work two jobs to ensure
that tuition, clothing, health care and every basic necessity
are provided for my children. My wife and I want them to
have everything that we had and more. We try to do things
together that we all enjoy doing. Once in a while we splurge
and buy something that they have desired for a long time.

A strange thing happens to us when we receive everything we want. We no longer appreciate the gifts given to
us. We live up to the old adage: "When you give people an
inch, they try to take a yard." I see it over and over again with
my own children. They are not content with the things they

have. They have no idea why they desire something. When we allow them to stay up later than their normal bedtime, the time we give them is never enough. Every possession fuels the desire for the next.

Many parents discover it is easier to say "yes." There are fewer battles and fewer arguments. But in many circumstances, there are greater benefits to refusing to give in. We never want our parents to disallow our deepest desires. But the word "no" can be a tool in shaping us as human beings. Denial can help us in the following ways:

1. It makes us appreciative of the things that we already possess and more importantly the people who have given us these things. When instant gratification becomes the norm, we use any means to acquire what we want. We practice the art of manipulation in order to get what we desire. Our sense of entitlement grows and we huff and puff like spoiled children when we are turned down. We often chase after the items that we do not really need. Once we get these things, we still experience an empty feeling because we desire them for the wrong reason. Author Samuel Johnson knew that our desire sometimes outweighed our need:

> The pleasure of expecting enjoyment is often greater than that of obtaining it, and the completion of almost every wish is found a disappointment.

By being denied of these things, we start to look at what we have and realize their importance and value to us. This assists us in truly developing a sense of priorities and character.

2. It helps us develop a work ethic and greater motiva-

tion. In our overindulgent society, we have fallen into the habit of constantly having our hand extended, wanting more. This has created material-obsessed individuals who have been robbed of the opportunity to learn of the joy of earning what we yearn for most. Nothing garners appreciation more than hard work.

3. Hearing the word "no" helps us in learning to manage disappointment. If our parents do not deny us, life certainly will. Hearing it first from a parent may help us to be better equipped to cope with the realities of life. There will be times when the word "no" will knock us off the tracks. It may be the rejection letter from the college on the top of our list or the refusal to our invitation to date that special someone that makes our heart sink.

The lesson of the child in Bethlehem shows how every person can overcome the denials of life. The parents of Jesus heard the word "no" many times as they sought a place to bring their baby into the world. They did not allow "no room at the inn" or "no place to lay their child's head" to interrupt the joy of bringing the Savior into the world. Instead, simplicity and humility became the way of life for the King of Kings.

The many times in which our parents took an alternative route to the easy way out and told us "no" are what helps us in overcoming these bumps in the road of life. They endured our tantrums and tears so that we could learn the value of patience and perseverance. Our parents did not need a crystal ball to see what was in our future. They could envision the days when disappointment would pull the rug out from underneath us. They understood how a simple two-letter word could form us into better people and teach us the lesson that the better things in life are worth waiting for. So next time your parents refuse to allow you to do as you wish, think about the long-term implications of their decision and reflect on how the word "no" is meant to show the deepest care and concern for you.

Your parents are smarter than you think

Young people often complain that their parents don't seem to understand what it is like being a teenager or a person in their young twenties. As a matter of fact, they believe that their parents don't seem to understand much of anything. Teenagers study their parents and wonder how these people who raise them are able to survive in the world. Writer Mark Twain wrote:

> When I was a boy of 14, my father was so ignorant
> I could hardly stand to have the old man around.
> But when I got to be twenty-one, I was astonished
> at how much he had learned in seven years.

As toddlers, our parents were superheroes to us. But as we enter our teenage years, we lose faith in the knowledge of our parents. When we emerge into our mid-to-late twenties, our perception of our parents changes. These thoughts were conveyed in a popular reflection called "The Images of Mother" (Author Unknown).

Four years of age: "My mommy can do anything!"

Eight years of age: My mom knows a lot! The whole lot!"

Twelve years of age: "My mother doesn't really know quite everything."

Fourteen years of age: "Naturally, mom doesn't know that, either!"

Sixteen years of age: "Mother? She is hopelessly old-fashioned!"

Eighteen years of age: "That old woman? She's way out of date!"

Age twenty-five: "Well she might know a little bit about it."

Age thirty-five: "Before we decide, let's get mom's opinion."

Age forty-five: "Wonder what mom would've thought about it?"

Age fifty-five: "Wish I could talk it over with mom."

As we enter the age of independence, the great battle begins. Our parents constantly interfere as we search to find our own way. We resent their meddling because we feel that we have all the pieces of life in place. At the marriage feast at Cana, Jesus seemed reluctant to oblige when His mother, Mary suggested that He should intervene when the host had run out of wine. He said to her, "Woman, how does your concern affect me? My hour has not yet come." His hour, the time of His public miracles, had not quite arrived, but Jesus immediately responded to her direction to the waiters when she urged, "Do whatever He tells you!" (Jn 2:1-11)

Throughout the years in which we think that we know it all, we take the care and concern of our parents for granted.

But as responsibility is stacked upon our plate, we start to realize that our parents were not always wrong. We suddenly awaken to see that the many years of dealing with essential family tasks have transformed them into people who are far more serious than we would like them to be. Successful entrepreneur Bill Gates reiterated this sentiment in an address he gave at a high school graduation:

> Before you were born, your parents weren't as boring as they are now. They got that way from paying your bills, cleaning your clothes, and listening to you talk about how cool you thought you are. So before you save the rain forest from the parasites of your parents' generation, try delousing the closet in your own room.

Your parents bear the weight of maneuvering through difficulties and finding solutions to everyday problems.

Wisdom has been forged from their experiences. The only way to learn about life is through living it. When we filter out our predisposed feelings of our parents, we may be enlightened by their years of existence. They have paid a price for their knowledge. They attempt to spare us from going through the same pain by preaching and lecturing us. By tuning them out, we may miss out on hearing some of the greatest pearls of advice. Remember that people only desire to become involved in your life when they truly care about you. Consider parental meddling an act of love. It is always easier to look the other way instead of becoming involved in your mistakes.

Next time you insist that you know it all, ask someone who can spare you from the pain of making the same mistakes as they did. Utilize the rich source of wisdom that your parents can provide. They are not as dumb as they look. Before making rash decisions, hear their side of the situation. You may be surprised by their suggestions. Appreciate them not only for the knowledge, but who they are. Cherish each conversation with them because there may be a day when they are not standing beside you. When times become difficult look to the ultimate family and ask for their help. Mother Teresa gave us this beautiful reflection:

> Heavenly Father,
> you have given us the model of life
> in the Holy Family of Nazareth.
> Help us, O Loving Father,
> to make our family another Nazareth
> where love, peace and joy reign.
> May it be deeply contemplative,
> intensely Eucharistic,
> revived with joy.
>
> Help us to stay together in joy
> and sorrow in family prayer.
> Teach us to see Jesus in the members of our families,
> especially in their distressing disguise.
> May the Eucharistic heart of Jesus
> make our hearts humble like his
> and help us to carry out our family duties
> in a holy way.
> May we love one another
> as God loves each one of us,

more and more each day,
and forgive each other's faults
as you forgive our sins.
Help us, O Loving Father,
to take whatever you give
and give whatever you take with a big smile.
Immaculate Heart of Mary,
cause of our joy, pray for us.

St. Joseph, pray for us.

Holy Guardian Angels,
be always with us,
guide and protect us.
Amen.

The Holy Family will guide you always!

You are what you eat, drink, read, watch and listen to

From the moment we are able to eat on our own, we are told by our parents to eat our vegetables. Our parents always seem obsessed with us receiving proper nutrition. We have been programmed to focus on food as the source of growth. We often hear, "You are what you eat!" But we must be aware of everything that we put into our body.

When my son received an iPod as a gift in the fifth grade, he asked if he could buy some songs on iTunes. Even though I relented, I explained some rules that he must follow if he would be allowed to search on his own for songs for his personal music player. I told Alex that any song with a little red box next to the title was off-limits. This box indicated that the song contained "explicit" lyrics. These songs, we agreed, were strictly forbidden.

My students often debate the effects of offensive lyrics, literature and programming. They shrug off these songs and shows as a form of harmless entertainment. They insist that these things have no effect on the way that we live. What they fail to understand is that as human beings we absorb the elements around us. Our brains act as video recorders that are imprinted with the images we see and hear. No matter how we try, it is impossible to filter out the things that influence us in a negative manner.

Modern media flaunts profanity, nudity and vulgarity at every opportunity. Even seemingly harmless shows are saturated with sexual innuendo and double entendres. Cartoons attempt to disguise a message far too mature for most young people to process. People often use the image of the frog in order to illustrate how we have been affected by the culture. If you placed a frog in a pot of boiling water, the frog would jump out immediately once it sensed danger. But if you put the same frog in a cool pot of water and slowly heated the water, the frog would succumb to the gradual heating of the water. The frog dies because it does not sense the impending danger of its surroundings. Our society immerses us into an atmosphere that seems harmless to us, but can kill us morally and spiritually. We can claim that we are immune to the culture. But like the frog, we cannot escape.

Many of the male students I teach make no apology for indulging in pornography. They argue that it is normal for a man to have the desire to see a naked woman. They believe that once the momentary pleasure ends, so too do the effects of the pornography. The images and video used for self-gratification change the way that we relate to each other. People no longer are objects of love, but rather objects of lust. We degrade them to mere objects that are used for our own pleasure.

Our surroundings convincingly change the way we act and think. We must be mindful of the negative influences around us. It is almost impossible to swim in jellyfish infested waters without getting stung. If we are not careful, the harmful aspects of our culture may sting us. Eliminate the things in your life that could erode your moral and spiritual well-being. Filter out vulgarity and obvious perversions with positive and virtuous living. The media takes the most important elements of humanity and makes them trivial. Shut off the shows that negatively impact the way you approach the relationships in your life.

Our culture highlights dysfunctional people and families because they shock us and grab our attention. The endless episodes of people arguing and screaming make us wonder what constitutes a normal relationship. We often avoid certain movies and shows because we feel uncomfortable watching them in mixed company. But how do these shows make us feel when we are alone? Do they awaken unhealthy feelings of lust? Do they use language that we would not use in formal and professional situations?

Sex is used as a lure. Advertisers use subtle and blatant images to make us notice a product. Movies and television dangle the hottest and most attractive stars so we will tune in to a certain show. Little emphasis is based on art and substance when the media knows that they can sell anything with sex. We witness the stars of our favorite movies and programs involved in empty sexual relationships. Since life imitates art in so many ways, we find ourselves mimicking their behavior unknowingly. When we see something so often, it no longer shocks us, so we start to condone certain attitudes and behaviors.

Our eyes and ears remain constantly ready to be our

instruments that witness the beauty and wonderful sounds around us. Since it is impossible to shut them off, we must avoid the things that are detrimental to us. Only the individual can change the channel, bypass a certain web site or turn off music with questionable lyrics. Censor the nonsense out of your world.

Although we are genuinely attracted to cutting edge entertainment that goes where no one else has gone, we should be aware when it crosses the line. Opt for leisure activities that enhance your life. Being mindful of the things that you watch, read and listen to does not have to mean that you must sit home and read your Bible each night as your only means of entertainment. There are many great alternatives. Do not rule out more wholesome programming. Choose to be educated as well as entertained.

In everyday living, we take food for granted. We fail to recognize its long term effects on the body and soul. We grab a quick bite to sustain us until we can eat again. Jesus gave us food that comes directly from heaven. Archbishop Fulton Sheen explained:

> The Eucharist is food for our soul, but the power of assimilation here belongs to Christ, and it is He Who, feeding us, unites us and incorporates us with His life. It is not Christ Who is changed into us, as is the food we eat; it is we who are incorporated in Him.　　　(*These are the Sacraments*)

If you are looking for wholesome nourishment, look no further than the Eucharist. You will receive everything that you need. It is the food that will transform you from the inside out.

Be aware of the atmosphere that surrounds you. Don't let it influence you in a negative way. Create your surroundings like you would decorate your home. Your world is like a garden, nurture it with care. Weed out the harmful things that can choke you spiritually. Maturity means that you have the freedom to choose what goes on your plate. Fill it with the items that will nourish your soul.

Reading will make you smarter

A student recently stopped by my office and asked if she could print a document from my computer. Since I was not working on my computer at the time, I agreed. As the young woman navigated her way on the web, I questioned her about her assignment. The student hesitated before admitting that she was printing a synopsis of the book that she should have read for the test that her class was taking that day. Before scolding the girl, I reflected on my own academic experience. During high school and college, I would avoid reading the books assigned at all cost. In fact, I avoided reading altogether. I utilized the synopsis of a book rather than experience the artistic treasure of the author. I squandered many opportunities to experience classics firsthand.

When my students discuss their strategy on how to complete assignments without doing the necessary reading, I talk to them about how they cheat themselves of not only becoming smarter, but of improving as human beings. Author Aldous Huxley said:

Every man who knows how to read has in his power to magnify himself, to multiply the ways in which he exists, to make his life full, significant and interesting.

Although most students believe that reading is an empty assignment given in order to keep them busy, it has incredible benefits.

We spend money on gym memberships and workout equipment, but we forget to exercise our mind. Reading keeps the brain active. The more we use our mind, the sharper it becomes. It enhances our memory. Reading changes the way that we think. In a frenzied world, reading assists us in improving focus. Sitting through a book requires a tremendous amount of concentration. Each time we open the pages of the book, we block out the world for the moment. Nothing matters but the material that sits in our hands. Our improved ability to focus will assist us in our daily living.

Reading also increases knowledge. Dr. Seuss poetically stated, "The more you read, the more you will know. The more you learn, the more places you'll go." Opening the book will also open doors. The things you learn when you read will never go to waste. The daily news, how-to books, and even the sports page will make you a welcome addition to any conversation. Do not be surprised if a job interview includes the question, "What was the last book that you read?" Others will find you more interesting as you unveil the knowledge that you have discovered in the articles and books that you have read.

Reading allows you to visit places where you have never been or know people that you have never met. The words on a page can amazingly transport us to another place or time.

Reading bridges the gap between the outside world and us. The process of reading can affirm our deepest thoughts and feelings. Theologian and author C.S. Lewis stated, "We read to know we are not alone."

If you want to expand your vocabulary, you should read as often as you can. The most articulate people are also the most avid readers. Reading exposes you to new words and vocabulary that you might not ordinarily use. Look to authors who were masters of language. They will give you a voice and a newfound command of words.

Reading expands your world as you expand your mind. It literally changes the way that you see the world. If you want to set yourself apart from fellow colleagues or students, read as often as you can. In your free time, open a book. Some people constantly insist that they are consumed by boredom. When you find yourself with nothing to do, read!

Recently when I walked through the library at school, I came upon a student who insisted he had nothing to do when I caught him goofing around. I was saddened that the student overlooked the gifts around him. Creative genius Walt Disney felt the same way saying, "There is more treasure in books than in all the pirate's loot on Treasure Island." Reach out for your gold today and read. Visit new destinations and open your mind to incredible possibilities.

Your life is not really all about you

From infancy our parents feed into our egocentrism. When we cried, they ran to our side. The slightest whimper commanded someone's attention. The world became our domain. We immediately believe that the world revolves around us. As we grow older, we consciously and maybe even subconsciously, live by the mantra "what's in it for me?" We naturally search for what is best for us in every situation. Although we may rationalize that our selfish tendencies will provide everything we need, it actually has the opposite effect.

I introduce every class I teach to psychologist and social philosopher Erich Fromm. In his thesis on relationships, *The Art of Loving*, Fromm speaks about the dangers of selfishness:

> The selfish person is necessarily unhappy and anxiously concerned to snatch from life the satisfactions which he blocks himself from attaining. He seems to care too much for himself, but actually he only makes an unsuccessful attempt to cover up and compensate for his failure to care for his real self.

We slowly learn that the more we give ourselves away, the richer we become. The shedding of our narcissistic cloak assists us in discovering the path to true happiness.

Many young people do spend much of their free time volunteering to help others in need. They are not interested in the money or the attention that they should receive. Instead, they receive the reward of self-satisfaction and the smiles of those that they are able to help. When we cultivate generosity with ourselves, we grow as human beings.

We have been created to love. Loving fulfills us and enhances who we are. Many people equate love with emotions. Love is much more than an emotion or a momentary feeling. It is the active care and concern for another human being. Love requires action, whereas emotions simply happen no matter what we do. It is impossible to love when we are wrapped up in our own narcissistic world. Loving others means that we should be aware of everyone around us. We must look and see who needs our attention. People who remain concerned only with themselves find it impossible to love.

The more people we meet, the more we discover that the world is a small place. Lines on a map separate one country from another. But no matter what language we speak, we are all, one humanity. We all desire the same thing: love. Our ability to care for one another is our most powerful gift. Every act of kindness is a ripple in the sea of humanity. We may see where it begins, but we have no idea where it ends.

We all have felt the effects of a loving gesture. Our disposition to assist others increases when someone helps us. The idea of "paying it forward" has been the subject of many movies because people understand the power of love. The objective of Jesus' earthly life was to get people to realize that the world can change with each act of love. Through His self-sacrifice, the world was transformed.

Christianity places an emphasis on our relationships. Jesus commanded us to love one another. This included those people we know or do not know. This dictum goes beyond the condition of whether we like people or they like us. This inter-connectedness should transform each moment of every day. Every word and action becomes significant. There is no room for the "me first" attitude in Christ's agenda.

When we place others at the forefront of our priorities, we unlock the secret of life. This idea was well conveyed in Charles Dickens' classic, *A Christmas Carol*. Ebenezer Scrooge had deteriorated as a person because he had forgotten the importance of love. The ghosts that visited the old miser showed him what was missing in his life. His conversion and total transformation only occurred because of his willingness to love the people in his life. Scrooge had an epiphany. Life was no longer about his money, his possessions, his selfishness or his thoughtless wishes.

Leave your cocoon of narcissism and shift your focus to those around you. The great paradox of taking care of others is that the person who reaches out ultimately benefits the most. The King of Kings spent His entire earthly life demonstrating how to find the secret of life by giving everything He had to others. Even though Jesus deserved our complete adoration, He catered to our every need. Renovate your own life by learning that your life is not about you.

Be not afraid!

We are accustomed to seeing worried faces on adults. The high-pressured executive, the overburdened mother, and the financially stressed may all demonstrate the anxiety that rests upon their shoulders. Today, many young people I know also seem to be affected by the weight of the world. Society expects children to grow up sooner than ever before. Playtime is substituted by responsibility and premature expectations. It is not unusual for parents to inquire about schooling even before their child is born.

Each year I witness students crumbling to the pressure. As they sit in my office and explain their situation, I realize that most of the anxiety is self-induced. Once the students become stuck within the cycle of worry, it is difficult to withdraw. We pile each care and concern upon the next until we find ourselves powerless to overcome them. As the Swedish proverb warns, "Worry gives a small thing a big shadow."

People are more fearful than ever. For those consumed by worry, I usually offer twofold advice: faith and action. The first step in easing anxiety is doing. This step requires us to be proactive. We must move from our paralyzed state and tend to the things that keep us from resting. We can move mountains with perseverance, but only one stone at a time.

We need to be realistic and change the things that are in our control. For the things that we can't, we must rely on another important dimension of our lives, faith. We should turn to the greatest self-help book ever written. In the Bible, those faced with uncertainty and dangers are given clear direction. They are told, "Be not afraid!" Whether it is the angel Gabriel speaking to Mary at the Annunciation or the risen Lord greeting His apostles, the advice is simple. When you are buried by grief and beleaguered by your trials, put your faith in God. Our Father in heaven wants us to surrender to His care. It should not surprise us that the phrase, "Be not afraid," occurs more than three hundred times in the Bible.

During his papacy, Pope John Paul II told the world many times to push aside fear. Whether he was addressing his fellow Poles who faced the perils of communism or young people who had to stand against the culture of death, his message was constant. John Paul was well aware that when we become involved in the daily affairs of this world, we often separate ourselves from God. With Christ besides us, fear vanishes.

In the Gospel of John, Jesus urged our true communion with Him:

> Remain in me as I remain in you. Just as the branch cannot bear fruit on its own unless it remains on the vine, so neither can you unless you remain in me. I am the vine, you are the branches. Whoever

remains in me and I in him will bear much fruit,
because without me you can do nothing. (Jn 15:4)

Jesus became one of us so that we could know Him personally. Our lives would be magnificent with Him, but help-
less without Him. Pope John Paul advocated our reliance
on Christ as we entered the new millennium: "Do not be
afraid, open wide the doors to Christ." He firmly understood
our tendency for self-sufficiency and how often we become
tangled with worry. We should invite Jesus into our lives.
The Pope stated:

> There is a temptation which perennially besets
> every spiritual journey and pastoral work: that of
> thinking that the results depend on our ability to
> act and to plan. God of course asks us really to co-
> operate with his grace, and therefore invites us to
> invest all our resources of intelligence and energy
> in serving the cause of the Kingdom. But it is fatal
> to forget that "without Christ we can do nothing"
> (cf. Jn 15:5).
>
> (*Novo Millennio Ineunte*, January 2001)

Once you feel the presence of God, the fear in your
world will lift. He is our greatest hope. With Jesus all things
are possible. He offers us salvation and the fear of this world
has no power over us once we join forces with Him. In the
days after the crucifixion, the apostles despaired because everything seemed lost. The appearance of Jesus and His reas-
surance put them at ease. When things are unraveling, listen
for His gentle voice. He speaks to you. "Be not afraid."

Always expect the unexpected

I recently announced a project that sent many of my students over the edge. Many hands were raised to express their displeasure. "Mr. Basile, don't you know about the other five projects that are due at the end of this month?" Although I sympathized with the plight of my young friends, I countered with the question of my own: "What will you do when you are faced with real problems that demand more than sitting in front of a computer to complete a few papers?"

Things may not be as bad as they seem when storm clouds appear. There are many days when you must put your life into perspective. I have often felt foolish after I spent time worrying about a problem when a more difficult situation took its place. We learn to plan our lives: our schooling, our finances, our careers, etc. But the more we attempt to set things in stone, the more things can change. Through my own experience, when I confidently thought that all of the pieces of life had fallen perfectly into place, reality has shown me otherwise. I often tell my students that, "We plan and God laughs." Many wise people in your life will tell you "when life gives you lemons, you must make lemonade." Your ability to rise above adversity will determine whether or not you will find sanity amidst the chaos.

The average person is challenged to transform the agony of life into extraordinary moments. What we do with adversity shapes us into what we become. You'll often see people on television or in the news that have started an organization to help others after a tragedy turned their own lives upside down. Suffering can help us see the world from a different perspective. We have come to understand the power of the hand that reaches into the storm cloud. We root for those who struggle to see light at the end of the very dark tunnel in which they are traveling. These people have come to understand that the gift of compassion heals us as we help others. When you find yourself confounded by problem after problem, look beyond yourself to discover consolation.

It is important not to allow difficulty to paralyze us. Helen Keller explained,

> When one door of happiness closes, another opens,
> but often we look so long at the closed door that
> we do not see the one which has opened for us.

Put yourself in the shoes of the Blessed Mother. From the moment she encountered the prophet Simeon, she waited for tragedy to arrive. Simeon had predicted the suffering long before it would happen. He told the young mother, "A sword would pierce your heart." From that instant Mary could have changed her outlook. She could have changed the way she lived. But she didn't. She realized that along with the sorrow would come unfettered joy.

We tend to grieve and focus on our disappointments

so often that we miss the other opportunities which present themselves to us. Look for the silver lining in those dark clouds. Search for the door that may lead to something better. Do not permit these disruptions to keep you from happiness.

Prepare for the worst so that you can deal with problems when they arise. Have an alternative plan so that you can move ahead even when obstacles attempt to derail you. The most experienced sailor learns never to trust calm seas, as he knows that storms can occur without warning.

It is important to learn the lesson that no matter what happens in life, no one can choose your attitude beside yourself. As we will see in the chapter on laughter, our ability to smile when life turns against us is the key to happiness. Look at the positive side of every situation. Search for the light of a new day and a fresh start. When life seems to be slipping away, grab a hold of your greatest treasure: the people you love. The strong bonds of your relationships will help you in almost any hardship. Allow others to share your joys and bear the weight of your suffering. Use each interruption and disruption in your life as a learning experience. C.S. Lewis explained:

> But pain insists upon being attended to. God whispers to us in our pleasures, speaks in our conscience, but shouts in our pains: it is His megaphone to rouse a deaf world.

Many people run from God when tragedy occurs. These are the opportunities to forge a lasting relationship with the Creator. Fall into His arms when you feel weakest. Make prayer a part of your daily experience now. Don't wait until the dark days to summon His assistance.

Let each moment shape your life and assist your growth as a human being. Just as the blowing sand and turbulent waters smooth the roughest rock, you, too, will be transformed by the difficult times in your life. Anticipate these situations before they arise. Expect the unexpected!

Communication comes in many forms. All are important!

People who study relationships preach about the essential element of communication. Communication is much more than the exchange of words between people. We assume that because we have spoken to others they comprehend our ideas, motives and intentions. It can be very frustrating when other people do not understand us as we attempt to explain something to them. George Bernard Shaw grappled with the difficulties in communication:

> The problem with communication is the illusion that it has occurred.

Miscommunication can cause rifts in our relationships. Constant communication can be exhausting. We tire of the arguments and the constant bickering. Instead of spending more of our precious time to get our point across, we may limit our verbal interaction with others.

We constantly monitor others and quietly assume their thoughts and motives. We study people and predict how they feel about us. We use casual glances and body language to determine their current mood. But no matter how proficient we become in studying others, there is no substitute for real communication. Sometimes we do not correctly articulate our true feelings. As writer Stephen King described:

> The most important things are the hardest to say, because words diminish them.

Real communication goes beyond simple language.

Modern e-mail enables us to broadcast our feelings and thoughts instantly around the world. It has replaced the art of letter writing when people sat with pen in hand and pored over each thought and phrase. The fast paced world demands that we blurt out an instant message without much thought. I personally have sent e-mails that I have later regretted. I believed I had conveyed my thoughts clearly; the recipient felt otherwise. Broadcaster Edward R. Murrow stood at the cusp of the technological age. Even then, he knew the dangers of the new communication era:

> The newest computer can merely compound, at speed, the oldest problem in the relations between human beings, and in the end the communicator will be confronted with the old problem, of what to say and how to say it.

The best communication takes time. Our words can literally get lost in translation. We must think before we speak in all situations. Some of the best conversations occur because someone edits their inner thoughts or saves what they have to say for another time.

I learned in the very first days of marriage it is not what you say, but how you say it. A rough tone or a hesitant phrase can be construed in a different way than we intended it. Be conscious of your body language when you speak to others. Crossed arms can demonstrate our lack of willingness to hear another's message. It can be difficult to gain the trust when eye contact is absent in communication.

Often, the greatest communicators are judged by their ability to listen. Give others a chance to tell their side of the story. It shows that we are taking the time to process what they have to say. When we permit the other person to speak, we may reveal a multitude of facts about what the other person is thinking. The slight hesitation to interject may even prevent us from saying something that will cause a problem.

Jesus illustrated the necessity of communication. Throughout the entire Gospel, Jesus created the time to communicate with others. The Kingdom of God would have remained the greatest secret if Jesus did not reveal it across the dinner table, on the street corner or in the sinner's den. Sure, He could always speak to the multitudes, but these intimate moments won over the most obstinate of hearts. The Creator of the world understood that nothing could connect two people more than eye contact and honesty.

Our family, friends, coworkers and classmates will not always know how we feel if we do not take the time to say it. We believe that mom knows that we love her "with all our heart" because she is constantly on our mind. Gaps in communication can be deciphered as apathy toward the relationship. A two-minute phone call or a quick visit can alter a person's perception of a relationship in an instant. The simple unselfish act of sacrificing time shows that we are willing to put some effort into our part of the relationship.

Never underestimate the difference between the sexes. Men and women approach relations and communication differently due to gender. A colleague gave me a copy of John Gray's book, *Men Are From Mars, Women Are From Venus*. Gray illustrates how the lives of women are rooted in emotion while men seek autonomy and self-sufficiency. It is a stereotypical look and certainly may not apply to everyone, but it does keep us mindful of the value of our interaction.

No matter how many words you use each day, you can become an expert communicator. Make the effort to get to know people. There is no substitute for real work. It will reward you with incredible dividends. Back up your words with your actions. Demonstrate your care and concern by sacrificing your time for the important people in your life. Others will know how you really feel by the things you do. Practice communication every day and it will lead to deeper relationships. It will bring greater value to your interaction and articulate the love that dwells within you.

Unplug and listen for the silence

With the advancement of technology, we have become very attached to our personal music devices, cell phones, portable DVD players and other various machines that fill the perceived void in our lives with music, movies and endless chatter. Each morning, teachers in our school must remind students as they enter the building to unplug from their toys in preparation for the class day. These devices have become the accessories for daily living. We seldom leave the house without the items that seem to bring us comfort and security. It is not unusual to see people driving to work and school immersed in deep conversations even though they are barely awake. As I stand in the hallway of my school each morning, I witness the hundreds of students who move to a soundtrack that plays through their earphones. The more we fall in love with the new technology, the more we forget about the value of silence. Artist Jean Arp expressed his dismay with this new trend:

> Soon silence will have passed into legend. Man has turned his back on silence. Day after day he invents machines and devices that increase noise and dis-

tract humanity from the essence of life, contemplation, meditation... tooting, howling, screeching, booming, crashing, whistling, grinding, and trilling bolster his ego. His anxiety subsides. His inhuman void spread monstrously like a gray vegetation.

The endless barrage of noise has overshadowed the necessity for peace and quiet. Our society has grown uncomfortable with the moments when we must listen to the voice deep within ourselves. Our stereos and televisions blast well into the night, until our weary bodies finally surrender to sleep.

Without silence, we can never grow spiritually. When I speak about spiritual growth, I am not just speaking about your relationship with God. Spirituality involves the understanding of who you are as a person. It revolves around the relationships in your life. It determines your emotional growth. We need reflection and contemplation to reveal the person that hides deep within the superficial layers that we show the world. Silence helps us to channel the true self and allows internal communication to occur.

Without peace and quiet, prayer is nearly impossible. When we pray, we speak to God. We desire to convey our deepest concerns, fears and hopes. The real goal of prayer is not to change God, it is to change the self. This process requires silence in order for true transformation. Mother Teresa urged that people seek contemplation in their search for the Lord:

> We need to find God, and he cannot be found in noise and restlessness. As the friend of silence, see how nature, trees, flowers, grass, grows in si-

lence; see the stars, the moon and the sun, how they move in silence... we need silence to be able to touch souls.

In the most stressful situations of His ministry, we witness Jesus withdraw and seek the consolation of peace and quiet. Solitude is necessary for mental health. Famous statesman William Penn explained, "True silence is the rest of the mind; it is to the spirit what sleep is to the body, nourishment and refreshment." It is no wonder that so many people recognize the external value of a quiet walk or retreat to gather their thoughts and pull the scattered pieces of life back together.

When we sit alone and reflect on our lives, reality finally emerges. We may not like what we see and feel. Reality is not always pretty. Change begins once we recognize the problems. When we tune out the world, we can never correct our imperfections.

Set aside time each day when you click off the television, iPod and cell phone. Use the quiet to rejuvenate your mind and soul. Listen to the voice within yourself. Discover what you really want and even more importantly, need. Spend time in reflection and prayer. Seek your God through heartfelt communication.

Thomas Merton was a Cistercian monk who wrote volumes about discovering the essence of God in the silence:

> The true contemplative is not one who prepares his mind for a particular message that he wants or expects to hear, but is one who remains empty because he knows that he can never expect to anticipate the words that will transform his darkness

into light. He does not even anticipate a special kind of transformation. He does not demand light instead of darkness. He waits on the Word of God in silence, and, when he is "answered," it is not so much by a word that bursts into his silence. It is by his silence itself, suddenly, inexplicably revealing itself to him as a word of great power, full of the voice of God.   (*The Climate of Monastic Prayer*)

We often feel as if we might miss out on something important if we shut down our technology even for a few moments. We never think about the things we may be missing instead. I recently had a conversation with a student that I caught texting during church. I had watched her from above in the choir loft. She looked at her phone dozens of times and sent numerous messages. "It was important that I contacted my friend!", she stated emphatically. She was content to stare blankly at the screen of her cell phone instead of placing herself in the presence of her God. We may miss out on even more if we do not seek silence.

The solitude of silence will open a new world within you. It can provide solace during the most chaotic times in your life and shelter you from the wild storms. Embrace silence and look at your world from a new perspective. Use the peace and quiet to contact the voice inside and your God above. Seek the silence.

Stop following the herd and think for yourself

Every child has begged their parents to do something because all of their friends were doing it. The cliché response of parents, "If everyone jumped off the bridge, would you jump off too?", has left many children standing in silence. We have often desired to join our friends in activities without much thought of why we actually want to do them. No one wants to be left out. We all yearn to be included. Standing alone on the sidelines is miserable.

In my sophomore year of high school, the seniors on our bus would think up a daily prank. One day, a scholar shouted from the rear of the bus, "Everybody up!" Without hesitation, every student on the bus stood. "Rock the bus!", he screamed next. "Left, right, left, right!" he continued. The entire body of the bus shifted as we sped along. Unaware that the driver was about to make a turn, we rocked more fervently. As we banked into the turn, the bus became airborne leaving only two wheels on the ground. We watched in horror wondering if our stupidity had caused us to flip the bus. Luckily, gravity brought the raised wheels back to the ground. The bus driver immediately pulled the bus to the curb to gain his composure. He then turned to the passengers of the bus to chastise the idiots that had almost caused a catastrophe. He called ahead to the school where the Dean of Discipline was waiting to greet us with a not-so-warm welcome.

I, along with every student on that bus, had followed blindly. In our efforts to be accepted by the rest of the crowd, we ignored common sense and the simple rules of safety. If someone had insisted that we ceased our lunacy, he may have been ridiculed, but he also may have made everyone else see the mistake that we were making. Breaking out of the box of conformity can put us in a lonely place. It takes an immense amount of courage to venture away from the pack.

The wiser members of society question why things are as they are. Bertrand Russell stated, "In all affairs it's a healthy thing now and then to hang a question mark on the things that you have long taken for granted." We are often content to follow the worn trail on the path because it saves us the trouble of carving one for ourselves.

You'll find yourself in many uncomfortable situations when others will expect you to join in the crowd. Someone may hand you a drink, a cigarette or drugs. Others may pull you into gossip. An invitation to partake in a certain activity does not indicate care and concern for you, but rather a desire to justify his or her actions. Remember that misery loves company. When everyone is involved, any action, no matter how reprehensible, seems acceptable. The Nuremberg trials that followed World War II held people accountable for the atrocities committed during the conflict. Many defendants declared that he or she was "only following orders." Even those who slaughtered thousands of people in the concentration camps blamed their actions on their superiors. Once we surrender our will to others for the sake of power, popularity or self-preservation, we also surrender our souls.

People despised Jesus because He broke the mold of conformity. He taught that He came to renew the world rather than be restricted by the rules created by men who did not understand the proper way to live. Do not be afraid to say and do what you please. But remember to stay on the moral path. What is right is not always popular and what is popular is not always right. If those around you really care for you, they will respect your decision to do what you want. Heed the advice of author Herman Melville: "It is better to fail in originality than to succeed in imitation." Allowing others to push you down the wrong road will neither bring you happiness nor popularity. Be a leader and carve your own path. Take control of your life. Think for yourself.

Learn moderation. Less is more

In the age of prosperity and affluence, Americans have subscribed to the philosophy: the bigger the better. We buy objects without thinking whether or not we really need them. We do not eat, drink and shop to live, but live to eat, drink and shop. Our hunger for material things can never be satisfied by our empty pursuit. We do not understand why others are content with their older cars, computers, and cell phones when sleeker, more attractive alternatives are available. We destroy ourselves by indulging in too much of a good thing. The habit of gluttony has infiltrated every aspect of living. The inner mechanism that tells us "enough is enough" has been shut down. We are a society of extremes. We have forgotten the lean years when people cherished the simplicity of spending time with family rather than searching for luxuries.

The average person "super sizes" everything they do. Fast food restaurants feature menus that allow us to gorge but leave us nutritionally empty. We often exclaim, "I'm starving!", but forget the real meaning of starvation and the many people that actually have to worry about where their next meal will come from. Most Americans have been spoiled by the plentiful bounty. We keep our stores open twenty-four hours a day so that the buffet will never close. We suppress the inner desire to leash our passions.

On a recent vacation to Florida, I spent the day at the beach next to some young people on Spring break. Around noon, they began to drink beer from the well-stacked cooler that they had brought with them. Soon after, they started drinking from a large funnel. One boy knelt in the sand while his friend poured the beer into the funnel, which traveled through a four-foot tube into his mouth. The two students repeated the ritual until they both passed out from the effects of the alcohol and the heat of the day.

As my students talk about their weekend exploits, I hear them mention funnels and games of beer pong. They have invented games that quicken the state of intoxication. The sport of drinking is used as a means of numbing existential frustration. When students hear that I attended a party, they believe that I indulged in the same mass consumption that they are accustomed to. My students scoff at me when I insist that even though I may enjoy different types of liquor the main objective is savoring the flavor of the drink. They assume that I share in their goal of reaching the delusional bliss of intoxication.

For those people who grow up in a European dining environment, beer and wine are accessible to everyone at the table. If a teenager chose to try the wine, he or she was given a small taste. My grandparents and parents desired to instill an appreciation for something created to complement the meal. Wine-making became a family tradition because of the important role of wine at the family table. Alcohol was not something to be slurped down without consideration for taste and enjoyment.

My parents taught me the virtue of temperance. My father worked as a telephone repairman in an affluent area of New York. He often brought home the objects that others had discarded because of minor flaws. Most of our bicycles had been thrown away by people who found it easier to buy new bicycles instead of fixing a flat tire. My parents stressed the importance of appreciating the items that we already owned and to avoid coveting objects that would never make us happy. They understood the power of temperance as St. Augustine did: Temperance restrains and silences the "passions which make us pant for those things which turn us away from the longing of God."

It is difficult to serve two masters. Unhealthy importance of material items can stand in the way of our relationship with God. Although the tangible goods of this world are easier to grasp onto than our invisible God, fight the urge of surrendering to earthly pleasures. Trim the fat out of your life. Eliminate the nonsense that keeps you from experiencing true joy. Avoid cramming your world with empty material that only leaves you hungry for more. Seek the practice of modesty. It bridles the passions that lead us to extremes.

Live by the minimalist philosophy where "less is more." Learn to savor the material goods of this world and use them to enhance your relationships. Leave the buffet while you still desire more and you will never tire of the material goods of the world.

Learn to love the person in the mirror

When I counsel students, I spend most of the time reassuring them that they possess the physical and mental attributes that they fail to recognize. I can certainly understand how they feel. I remember staring in the mirror as a teenager wondering if there would be anyone out there in the world who could fall in love with me. Away from the mirror, nothing I did seemed good enough. There was always someone who excelled where I did not. I felt inferior to other people my age. It is normal for a young person to experience doubt.

We tend to be our own toughest critics. Even when our family and friends praise us, we still doubt our abilities. We have been taught to avoid excessive pride and vanity. Because of this, we downplay our best qualities. We confuse self-love with narcissism and selfishness.

There is no greater boost to self-esteem than practicing generosity. Giving yourself to God and others will do wonders to your confidence and image. We see life from a new vantage point and feel good about ourselves when we break out of the world of egocentrism. We begin to appreciate ourselves as people recognize our willingness to reach out to those in need.

Spending time in prayer and contemplation provides a clearer vision of our role in this world. It is no wonder that spending time in church makes us feel differently about ourselves. An active faith life paves our place in this world. Being part of God gives us the courage to do anything. There is no better way to improve your self-image than to see yourself in the reflection of the Creator.

Take notice of your greatest gifts and talents. Everyone has strengths and weaknesses. Devoting time to your true passions will assist you in realizing your genuine abilities. Stop being modest and display your gifts to others. Not everyone can do what you do. This is what makes your talent even more special. Do not be afraid to learn something new. Hidden talents lie beneath the surface waiting to be discovered. Enjoy your successes. Reward yourself for hard work and special achievements. When you minimize your success, other people may have a hard time giving you praise that you deserve. Let your light shine for the world to see.

Try to avoid judging others. The most critical people are usually the ones who are not content with their own self-image. Gossip occurs because it is easier to tear someone else apart instead of improving ourselves. Praise others on the things that they do well. Build them up and share in the glory of their accomplishments. Counsel him or her on the items that need improvement in a gentle manner. Learn from the errors of others and use them to work on your own self-improvement.

When life does not go as planned, don't blame yourself. Many young people bury themselves with guilt and self-doubt. This only makes our situations worse. Some circumstances cannot be changed. Smile and stay positive. Be gentle on yourself. Become your greatest supporter rather than your own worst enemy. Do not take everything personally. Even though we may feel as if the world is against us, it could be that we, ourselves, are the main obstacles that stand in the way of true happiness.

Make an effort to look at yourself today with appreciation and love. Learn to love the person that stares back at you in the mirror. It is impossible to love others if we do not love ourselves first. Develop the person that sets you apart from others. Be yourself and people will appreciate you for who you are.

Money never guarantees anything

In our school, the juniors research their family history as part of a yearlong project. Since America is a country of immigrants, many of these students have had a discussion with their relatives on why they desired to come to this country. I ask my students to share the results of their research and explain the goals and dreams of their ancestors. Most students state that their relatives came to America to find employment and economic stability. My two grandfathers left farms in Italy and Ireland because their economic situation presented no other option. Shortly after passing through Ellis Island, both of these men enlisted in the Army. American citizenship was so sacred to them that they were willing to sacrifice everything, including their lives.

If we asked our ancestors their definition of the word "success," they probably would have stated that success is measured in the love of family, a safe comfortable place to live, and job stability. But as each generation attempts to surpass the last, we redefine the word "success." Today we measure the level of success on how much fame and fortune a person attains.

Our ancestors sacrificed everything for the American dream, which was defined as the freedom to work hard in a country where anything was possible. Today, the American dream has morphed into a desire for celebrity and wealth. People risk it all for fifteen minutes in the spotlight. With a dollar and a dream, we stand in line to purchase a lottery ticket that will make us instant millionaires.

We are conditioned from the moment that we enter school to study so that we can excel. Good grades will help us to get into a prestigious college, which in turn land us a good job and a lucrative career. Money quickly becomes the bottom line. Somewhere along the path of our journey, we overlook the importance of fulfillment and happiness. Salary supersedes joy and passion. In our pursuit to discover the pot of gold at the end of the rainbow, we foolishly put more importance on the reward than the task we must perform every day.

Choose a career that makes you long for Monday morning. There is nothing worse than dreading the buzz of the alarm clock that propels us into another day of boredom and misery. Do not permit a salary to be the determining factor in choosing a certain profession. Being involved in a career that inspires you can be the difference in whether or not you find fulfillment.

The lure of a fancy car and luxurious home heightens our appetite for money. We see others and their possessions and we believe that if we owned the same item, our lives would change instantly. You only need to observe the lifestyles of the rich and famous in Hollywood to understand that money can inhibit our pursuit of true happiness.

In your hunt for real wealth, look to the relationships in your life. Your career, bank account and stock portfolio mean absolutely nothing without others to share in them. The love that you share will pay dividends that will last a lifetime and far exceed any other investment. When Jesus stated that it was "easier for a camel to pass through the eye of a needle than for a rich man to enter the kingdom of heaven," He wanted us to grasp the dangers of placing money over God and others in the Kingdom. The desire for God is often dissolved in the pursuit of earthly goods. Put a correct priority on material possessions. Use your accumulated wealth to shower others with kindness.

You can hit the jackpot by investing your time into love. You will grow richer than you ever imagined.

If we couldn't laugh, we would all go insane

As I explained earlier in the book, the older we get, the more serious we become. I recently sat on an airplane and reflected on how differently I felt since my first flight over thirty years before. I could not block out the numerous news specials on air safety. Gone was the pure exhilaration and anticipation of traveling to a new place. Instead, I was a much more serious passenger. Each creak and squeak made me wonder if our flight was going as planned. Our expansive knowledge increases the amount of worry because we are aware of everything that can go wrong.

I borrowed the title for this chapter from the Jimmy Buffett song, "Changes in Latitude":

> It's those changes in latitude, changes in attitude,
> nothing remains quite the same.
> With all of our running and all of our cunning.
> If we couldn't laugh, we would all go insane.

Jimmy Buffett has made a living looking at life from the lighter side. His clever lyrics often urge the listener to avoid the stress of living to discover any way you can to smile. As children, we laughed constantly. We found even the silliest things humorous. As life evolves, we overlook the importance of a good chuckle. Instead, we obsess about the next deadline and paying the latest bills. The value of laughter goes well beyond enjoying the moment.

Laughter strengthens our relationships. It creates a special bond with others. People often recall the more enjoyable moments that they have shared together. Entertainer Victor Borge said, "Laughter is the closest distance between two people." Humor instantly connects people. It breaks down the barriers that we place between ourselves and others.

People are attracted to the person that laughs. The best speakers often begin a presentation with a joke or anecdote. The "life of the party" is usually surrounded by people who simply want to forget momentarily about the tribulations of life. Laughter is a magnet that draws people to us.

Humor often defuses conflict. It provides a temporary pause so we can change the momentum of an awkward moment. Laughter reverses the direction of the downward spiral. Comedian Bob Newhart proposed, "Laughter gives us distance. It allows us to step back from an event, deal with it and move on." When we remain immersed in a tense environment, we may regret the actions that follow. A good laugh will assist us in overcoming frustration.

Try to find the positive side of every situation. Learn to laugh at even the most humiliating and frustrating moments. Things will suddenly not seem as bad. Sometimes we must laugh at ourselves before the rest of the world does. Laughter has incredible power. It infuses sunshine into the bleakest moments. Even when it seems as if we are defeated, our greatest weapon as Mark Twain reminded us, is laughter. I never doubt the studies that proclaim that those who laugh the most live longer. Stress immediately fades when laughter begins.

There will be many times when our ability to laugh will be the only way to initiate joy into an otherwise gloomy period in our lives. In *Man's Search for Meaning*, his book that recalled his imprisonment in Auschwitz, Viktor Frankl reminds us that our ability to choose our attitudes is the last human freedom. He knew that the only way to survive was to find humor in the tragic and absurd. When you think that life has sent you into a freefall, remember laughter is your parachute. Never hesitate to let a good chuckle ease your fall.

A sin is more than something to keep you from entering heaven

Every religion teacher eventually teaches a lesson on the Ten Commandments. The "Decalogue" or "Law" was given to Moses by God on Mount Sinai. As I explain the guidelines that God has given us to assist us in our relationship with Him and others, students urgently desire to discuss whether or not a particular sin will keep them from entering heaven. I mentioned earlier in the book how our society tries to beat the system by searching for loopholes. Our approach is the same when it comes to sin.

We tend to evaluate sin as a blemish that appears on our personal transcript. Willing to do anything to erase it, we try to rationalize it away. Sin bothers us, but not for the reasons that it should. Sin has been defined as "an utterance, a deed or a desire contrary to the eternal law" (CCC, 1849) and "an offense against God" (CCC, 1850). Sin destroys our relationship with God and others. It keeps us from truly loving as we should. It serves as a roadblock to real, honest communication. Sin isolates us in our world of selfishness. It entices us to neglect others. Sin erodes the soul as it deteriorates the bonds that fulfill us as human beings.

During the greatest act of sacrifice and mercy, the passion and death of Jesus, the evil of humanity demonstrated how it can act when immersed in self-absorption. As Jesus shows us how to love, Satan contradicts the actions of our Lord with various displays of sin. The cast of Good Friday tended to their own selfish agenda as God's Son gave away everything He had.

Temptation causes us to stray from our mission to love one another as Jesus taught us. If seduction becomes impossible to resist, then we must eliminate it from our lives. Jesus offered this advice to His disciples:

> If your right eye causes you to sin, tear it out and throw it away. It is better for you to lose one of your members than to have your whole body to go into Gehenna. And if your right hand causes you to sin, cut it off and throw it away. It is better for you to lose one of your members than to have your whole body go into Gehenna...   (Mt 5:29-30)

Jesus is not encouraging self harm, but instead He is urging us to eliminate the objects or people that cause us to sin. If you have individuals in your life that steer you away from goodness and truth it may be time to part company; if your cell phone has become a device for gossip and detraction (the spreading of harmful information that lessens a person's character and reputation) it may be time to limit its use; if you find yourself wandering to a place on the internet that demeans the value and beauty of sexuality, it may be time to stay away from the computer unless you need to utilize it for its vast resources.

Most people are acquainted with the Seven Deadly Sins or Capital Sins, as they are also known. The Church cites these as the chief sources of sin. The capital sins can be defined as follows:

1. **Pride**: The unhealthy infatuation with our own ability. We choose to promote ourselves even if it means that we turn away from God and others.
2. **Greed** (covetousness): We place a great importance on worldly possessions. We lose perspective of our heavenly goals when tied to material things.
3. **Lust**: Excessive desire for sexual pleasure at any cost. The value of the human being is lost in this unhealthy desire.
4. **Anger**: Excessive and unjustified emotion towards another. Hatred controls our actions when it consumes us.
5. **Gluttony**: An excessive desire for food, drink and material possessions. The more we consume, the less we are fulfilled.
6. **Envy**: We display sorrow when others experience good fortune. Any feeling of charity is lost as we seek to take away from their joy at any cost. Instead of support, we resort to detraction and slander.
7. **Sloth**: Laziness of the body and mind. We refuse to act because of the cost of time and talent. We turn our backs on God and others when we neglect our physical and spiritual duties.

God knows that we make mistakes. It is for this reason that He sent us His Son. The mission of Jesus focused on reconciliation and forgiveness. He wants us to learn from our mistakes and improve the quality of our lives as we evolve into good people. Every transgression should be countered with an act of selflessness and love. Each misstep should bring us closer to Christ through working on perfecting our souls.

The question of sin and heaven also weighed heavily on the minds of His disciples. They asked the Teacher how to attain eternal life. Jesus' response was simple:

> When the Son of Man comes in his glory, and all the angels with him, he will sit upon his glorious throne, and all the nations will be assembled before him. And he will separate them one from another, as a shepherd separates the sheep from the goats. He will place the sheep on his right and the goats on his left. Then the king will say to those on his right, "Come, you who are blessed by my Father. Inherit the kingdom prepared for you from the foundation of the world. For I was hungry and you gave me food, I was thirsty and you gave me drink, a stranger and you welcomed me, naked and you clothed me, ill and you cared for me, in prison and you visited me." Then the righteous will answer him and say, "Lord, when did we see you hungry and feed you, or thirsty and give you drink? When did we see you a stranger and welcome you, or naked and clothe you? When did we see you ill or in prison, and visit you?" And the king will say to them in reply, "Amen, I say to you, whatever you did for one of these least brothers of mine,

you did for me." Then he will say to those on his left, "Depart from me, you accursed, into the eternal fire prepared for the devil and his angels. For I was hungry and you gave me no food, I was thirsty and you gave me no drink, a stranger and you gave me no welcome, naked and you gave me no clothing, ill and in prison, and you did not care for me." Then they will answer and say, "Lord, when did we see you hungry or thirsty or a stranger or naked or ill or in prison, and not minister to your needs?" He will answer them, "Amen, I say to you, what you did not do for one of these least ones, you did not do for me." And these will go off to eternal punishment, but the righteous to eternal life.

(Mt 25:31-46)

On which side will you fall, the left or the right? Each time we prepare to act, we should ask ourselves, "How will my actions affect others?", and "Am I looking to benefit other people or only myself?" Sin blooms with the fertilizer of selfishness, but it is uprooted by love. Keep others in mind when you make your decisions. Look for Christ within everyone you meet. Do not let sin be the obstacle to true loving relationships. Learn from each mistake and let it be a lesson on how to look more deeply. Stop focusing on sin and keep your eye on virtue instead.

Every teacher gravitates to the great teachers. We want to find other educators who really understand how to convey the deepest life lessons. It was no surprise that immediately after Pope John Paul II died, people began referring to him as "John Paul the Great."

He loved young people. When he entered a room, auditorium or stadium, young people cheered. They felt a kinship with this older man. They sensed his love of God. They wanted to pray like him. They desired to feel the presence of Christ like he did. When John Paul spoke, he never lectured. He gently pointed their young hearts to Jesus. At World Youth Day in 1993, he once again made an impact with all those who listened:

> Do not be afraid to go out on the streets and into public places, like the first Apostles who preached Christ and the Good News of salvation in the squares of cities, towns and villages. This is no time to be ashamed of the Gospel (cf. Rm 1:16). It is the time to preach it from the rooftops (cf. Mt 10:27). Do not be afraid to break out of comfortable and routine modes of living, in order to take

up the challenge of making Christ known in the modern "metropolis." It is you who must "go out into the byroads" (Mt 22:9) and invite everyone you meet to the banquet which God has prepared for his people. The Gospel must not be kept hidden because of fear or indifference. It was never meant to be hidden away in private. It has to be put on a stand so that people may see its light and give praise to our heavenly Father (cf. Mt 5:15-16).

Jesus went in search of the men and women of his time. He engaged them in an open and truthful dialogue, whatever their condition. As the Good Samaritan of the human family, he came close to people to heal them of their sins and of the wounds which life inflicts, and to bring them back to the Father's house. Young people of World Youth Day, the Church asks you to go, in the power of the Holy Spirit, to those who are near and those who are far away. Share with them the freedom you have found in Christ. People thirst for genuine inner freedom. They yearn for the Life which Christ came to give in abundance. The world at the approach of a new millennium, for which the whole Church is preparing, is like a field ready for the harvest. Christ needs laborers ready to work in his vineyard. May you, the Catholic young people of the world, not fail him. In your hands, carry the Cross of Christ. On your lips, the words of Life. In your hearts, the saving grace of the Lord.